Raised in a quaint Utah town by an English teacher mother and a dairy farmer father, Adria Morris Arafat embarked on a journey marrying a Palestinian partner over four decades ago. With a master's degree in education, Adria has dedicated over 25 years to teaching ESL, enriching the lives of countless students. Steering educational institutions, she served as a principal in private Islamic schools for five years. Fuelled by an insatiable wanderlust, she finds solace and inspiration in not only traversing the globe, but living in those places as well as weaving cultural nuances into her writing.

To my wonderful and spectacular life tourist, my husband Aiman.

Adria Morris Arafat

THE PALESTINIAN TOURIST

AUSTIN MACAULEY PUBLISHERS

Copyright © Adria Morris Arafat 2024

The right of Adria Morris Arafat to be identified as author of this work has been asserted by the author in accordance with sections 77 and 78 of the Copyright, Designs and Patents Act 1988.

All rights reserved. No part of this publication may be reproduced, stored in a retrieval system, or transmitted in any form or by any means, electronic, mechanical, photocopying, recording, or otherwise, without the prior permission of the publishers.

Any person who commits any unauthorized act in relation to this publication may be liable to criminal prosecution and civil claims for damages.

All of the events in this memoir are true to the best of author's memory. The views expressed in this memoir are solely those of the author.

A CIP catalogue record for this title is available from the British Library.

ISBN 9781035871476 (Paperback)
ISBN 9781035871483 (ePub e-book)

www.austinmacauley.com

First Published 2024
Austin Macauley Publishers Ltd®
1 Canada Square
Canary Wharf
London
E14 5AA

I would like to thank my family first and foremost for providing all the wonderful stories, my husband for pushing me to finish this even after years of not writing, and Aunt Carroll for giving the book a once over that it desperately needed. But especially, the people of Gaza. They are the most resilient and brave people I know. May God help and protect them all.

Part One

June 1984

I could have kissed him. I didn't know his name or anything about him, but I really could have kissed a total stranger. They say there is something about a man in a uniform, but that wasn't it. It was the fact that I was home. I mean really home. I could hear English everywhere. I could understand what people were saying. I could have kissed him.

I didn't, of course. What I did do was buy the most expensive hamburger in my life. I spent $10 to buy a burger. Of course, those were airport prices, but I was home. And I needed a taste of home to wash out the bad taste in my mouth from the previous 48 hours. It felt like I had been to hell and back. But I can't go back just 48 hours; I have to go back to the beginning.

October 1982

As I was walking up the path to my dorm, I could hear the music. I could hear the music all the way across the parking lot. It was very loud. It was disco. It was the 80s.

Even though it was supposed to be a 'Halloween' dance, not many people were in a costume. I showed up dressed as a waitress; a big stretch there. I was a waitress just getting off work. I walked home from the little Chinese restaurant around the corner from my dorm. I was in my second year at the local college. It was a pretty typical college town replete with the mandatory football teams/basketball teams that everyone supported. We even had a multimillion-dollar dome that was used for everything from basketball to music concerts. It was an hour away from where I grew up and might as well have been on the moon as far as my family was concerned. I don't remember them ever coming up for a visit. To save money, I lived in the dorms. To save even more money, I lived in a dorm where I could cook my own meals. Men lived on the first floor; women lived on the second and third floors. I had five roommates and had to share my bedroom with another girl. My roommate was actually a local girl trying to get away from her family. Sound familiar?

I didn't know it, but that Halloween dance would change the entire course of my adult life. At the time, it was a distraction from an otherwise typical and boring life. I loved the music—Donna Summer, Devo, Wham, Air Supply, Lionel Richie, and Kenny Rogers. My taste in music was very eclectic. My mom liked rock and roll; my dad liked country. I listened to everything in between.

I ran out onto the floor when they played a song I really liked and didn't care that I didn't have a partner. The only people there were the people who lived in the dorm, and I knew them all, so what the hell. I came off the dance floor—the lobby of my dorm—and stood leaning on the railing debating whether I should go up and get out of my stinky clothes or not.

I heard a voice say something about dance. I looked around in disbelief. Was he asking me to dance? Sure enough, he led me onto the dance floor. We danced like we were young wild things. We were young wild things. Then they played a slow song. I wasn't about to grab onto some guy I had just met. I mean I still smelled like bad Chinese takeout. The next song was a fast one—good. Not good. He stood like a statue, a Greek statue to be sure. He was tall, dark, handsome, and mysterious—he didn't live in my dorm because I would have remembered a Greek God. Another fast song played. He didn't move. At least he didn't ask another girl to dance.

I had to make my move. I walked over to him and said, "You're a good dancer." How lame is that? Damn, I couldn't come up with anything wittier than that? To my shock and amazement, he took the hint, and we went back out onto the dance floor. We closed down the bar, I mean the dorm. Dancing is a very expressive form of communication. I don't remember saying two words the whole night. We danced the entire night together.

At the end of the night, we were both so sweaty and out of breath that we could hardly talk. A girl who lived in the dorm was an amateur photographer and she asked if she could take our photo. She was in her black-and-white phase, but it is one of my most cherished possessions—a photo of the night I met him!

I couldn't even dance a slow dance with this guy, so how to end a night of endless dancing? A kiss, a hug, and in the end, it was a handshake. I floated to my room. I couldn't wait to call my mom the next day. We had a system, so I didn't have to pay for the call. I would call collect and ask to speak to myself, my mom would say I wasn't available, and then she knew I was in my room, and she would call me back. A cheap, but efficient way to get Mom to pay and to talk to me. I was a poor college student, what can I say?

"How's everything with you and Dad?" I asked.

Mom replied, "Your father is off running around with his horses." That was how our conversations went. But this time I could hardly contain myself. "Mom, I've met a man with shoulders." I know how silly that sounds, but when you are surrounded by geeks, and skinny guys your own height, it really means something.

I had tried dating a bit at college. Not one of my better ideas by the way. Usually, they were only interested in being your friend or a friend with benefits. I wasn't interested in either of those options. The guys who lived in my dorm were mostly from far-off places and didn't like the food offered in the cafeteria. They wanted to be able to eat food from home—Vietnam, Nigeria, Russia, Yugoslavia, and Bangladesh.

I hadn't paid much attention to the origin of my fellow dormies. These guys from Vietnam, and Nigeria were crazy about ping pong. I had never paid that much attention to them at all. They played on the ping pong table (on the dance floor) in my dorm. I came home from my afternoon class and didn't feel like going upstairs. One of my roommates was sitting on a couch so I went over to talk to her about the dance the night before. I was in the middle of explaining how I met this tall mysterious guy, when who should walk through the doors. I must have been six shades of red, but he was very nice and didn't say anything. In point of fact, he walked over to the ping pong table without giving me even so much of a glance.

I followed him over to the table. He had to wait his turn, and again I started the conversation, "I had a good time last night."

He nodded politely, and said, "They call me a Palestinian tourist."

I said, "Of course, they do, you aren't from here."

He shook his head in disbelief, "No, I mean they call me a tourist. They say we are bad people."

I must admit, my geography was a bit sketchy, but my political science knowledge was worse. I grew up in a very small town in rural Utah of all places. All I knew about Palestine was what I had heard from the American news channels—they were bad people who sometimes hijacked airplanes. Palestine was far away in a place called the Middle East. I had spent the summer before my senior year in high school reading about Middle Earth but didn't have a clue about the Middle East.

He really meant they called him a 'terrorist.' I was a bit slow on the uptake. "You're not a terrorist, you're a student," I said. It was his turn to play ping pong so this conversation would have to wait.

I had sort of been watching the other guys play. The Nigerian player was very good. He was fast and sure of his shots. I had no idea if my 'tourist' could play or not, but we were about to find out. I admit, I hadn't played much ping pong in my life, but I did have an eye for sports. How could I not with a softball-playing father, and a younger brother who played every sport imaginable and every Sunday spent worshipping at the foot of the Television Church of Sports? Monday nights were almost as holy. Are you ready for some ping pong?

Boy, could he play! He had some moves I had only seen on sports specials. He could more than hold his own with these guys. My only move was to ask him to come back and watch our nightly ritual of M.A.S.H. We faithfully watched it every night after the local nightly news downstairs in the lobby as we didn't even have a T.V. in our dorm room.

This was our routine. I would go to class, come home, watch him play ping pong for hours, then watch MASH, then go to bed. We started off talking about mundane everyday things: family, likes, dislikes, and classes. It couldn't have been very in-depth as his English was terrible. I remember gesturing a lot. I remember laughing even more.

One night, the cafeteria in another dorm that he always ate from was having a prime rib dinner. I was very excited as this felt like a date. Except that he had shown up with his roommate in tow. Ok, not a date, just an outing with friends. We got in line, and I spent most of the time talking with his roommate. The roommate's English was much better. When we got to the station with the prime rib, my two companions had the most horrified looks on their faces. I couldn't imagine what was wrong. The roommate explained that we didn't eat 'blood.' I tried to explain that what they could see wasn't actually blood but was stained from the blood. Real blood would have congealed and gone black. My limited experience with trying to explain congealed and non-congealed blood to a non-native speaker was a complete failure. They compromised by taking an end cut of the prime rib, and I stuck with my 'bloody' piece. It was all they could do to not upchuck on their plates.

My knowledge of why it wasn't blood had been gained from growing up on a farm where we occasionally killed our own dinner; be it a chicken, pig, or wild animal. It wasn't strange to open the fridge and find a huge chunk of lard on the bottom shelf, fresh eggs that gave double yolks in the door, and packages of wild game in the freezer. When I say wild game, I mean wild: geese, pheasants, deer, and even elk.

I have fond memories of going camping/hunting with my dad. My mom wasn't that much of a camper, but she would come along and keep an eye on the camp while we all went off hunting. One year in particular sticks in my mind. We had invited a couple to come along with us to our favorite hunting spot. It was on top of a mountain so getting there was more challenging than hunting an elusive buck. Once we were ensconced in the middle of the quaking aspens, we set off in search of the elusive 'Cervidae'—white-tailed deer. The men were charging down a gorge after being dropped off by a truck, and I was with the wife walking halfway down the ridge. I wouldn't know how far down we really were until later.

Walking along, we were talking and laughing and not really paying attention until we were confronted by a buck who had been scared up from the bottom by the men. We were both so surprised that she almost didn't get the shot off. But she actually shot the animal. The men were yelling at us, but we couldn't hear them, and they couldn't hear us. They kept walking to camp. She looked at me and I looked at her. It was up to me to walk back to camp and get help. Needless to say, by the time I walked into camp, they had figured that we had either shot a deer or were lost. I said the obvious—we weren't lost, and why didn't they come to help? They replied that hadn't heard us, and figured we were headed back to camp. Pointless to say, we all piled into the truck, and I tried to remember where I had left her. The road was far from where we had shot the deer being on the top of the ridge, but we eventually found her halfway down the hill. I will never forget how long it took to drag a dead deer up the hill side. But the pride and joy we felt being the only ones to have shot an animal lasted the entire trip. Back to dinner in the dorm.

Nonetheless, my dinner companions enjoyed their baked potato more than the prime rib. I had tried to extol the virtues of medium rare but to no avail. The night wasn't a complete disaster though; I had been introduced to the roommate. I didn't understand how profound this was. I didn't understand a lot of things. But I did know one thing. The more I talked with my 'tourist.' the more I liked him. I first liked his shoulders; big, broad, muscular shoulders. He stood about half a foot taller than me, so my head fit right under his chin on his broad chest. I liked how he made me laugh. He was forever trying to make me laugh. It wasn't stupid jokes or making fun of someone either. It was always witty and clever.

We could talk for hours. We talked for hours. Sometimes we would look up and around and find it was the middle of the night and everyone had gone to bed. We had talked for God knows how many hours straight.

November 1982

Thanksgiving had always been a big deal in my house. Sometimes I think it was bigger than Christmas. I remember one year going up to southern Idaho, where my maternal grandparents lived as my paternal grandparents were both dead. Grandma made one of her famous turkey dinners—my brother ate himself sick. I mean he ate so much that he was rolling on the floor writhing in pain. It was all we could do not to laugh. I probably did anyway. It was also a time when my father, having stuffed himself only a few hours earlier, would be in the kitchen hacking on the turkey carcass to make his infamous miracle whip and turkey sandwich. It just wasn't Thanksgiving until Dad had a sandwich.

Meanwhile, back in the dorms.

I had to go home for the holiday. I didn't have work as the Chinese restaurant closed for the holidays, and I didn't have a good excuse not to go home. As usual in Utah in November, it snowed. There was a nice blanket of wet sticky snow all over the cars and the road as I got up that morning to drive home. My 'tourist' was coming to say goodbye to me but got sucked into a snowball fight. It wasn't his first, but it was one of the best I've ever been in. In a few minutes, the whole area was full of crazy cold college students flinging snowballs at anything that moved. I really needed to get going and honked and waved him over. He kissed me goodbye on the cheek. He kissed me. It was my cheek, but it was a kiss. That was all I remember about that Thanksgiving.

Christmas 1982

I wasn't going home for Christmas. All my roommates were leaving, and I was going to be alone, but I didn't care. I wanted to keep my job, and that meant staying for the whole two weeks. No roommates, no classes, no one around, anyone remember Risky Business? Dah dah dah dah dah dah dah…just take those ol' records off the shelf…Ok, so I didn't run around in my shorts and socks, but I could have. Instead, I spent the whole two weeks with my 'tourist.' We spent every waking minute together, except when I was working. Talking, walking, driving, and talking some more. We talked about everything.

He explained about his life and his family. He had grown up in Gaza City. His family was from the city as opposed to being refugees. His family has been there for as long as anyone can remember—hundreds if not thousands of years. In point of fact, his full name bears his father, grandfather, great-grandfather, great-great-grandfather, great-great-great-grandfather, and even great-great-great-great-grandfather's name. Talk about genealogy! They don't just pay it lip service; they know it by heart. He is the oldest of eight children, and the oldest boy. Why would that be so significant you ask? Because the tradition is that the oldest son should name his first boy after his father. So, he already knew what his son's name was going to be. That was okay by me as I knew what my first daughter was to be named too. I had my own family tradition to uphold. What's good enough for the gander is good enough for the goose.

I had a couple of days off and really didn't want to go home, so we drove up to see my grandparents. I hadn't gone up to Idaho for Thanksgiving, so this was a good time to visit. Of course, I would sleep in one bedroom and he on the couch hide-a-bed.

My grandfather took one look at him and approved whole heartedly. My grandfather's opinion was one I held in very high regard. I had gone to live at my grandparent's home the day after I graduated from high school. It was my way to 'break away' without any conflict. They were very gracious and took me in like the stray puppy I was. I was independent enough but with supervision. I could come and go as I pleased, and they got me a very good job working where they worked—at McDonald's. Grandma was one of the best cashiers they had. This was long before electronic cash registers. You had to know the prices and add everything up on paper. Hell, you had to give correct change without the machine telling you how much to give back! She and I could handle an entire bus on its way to Yellowstone National Park in 20 minutes flat! Those were good times.

Grandpa was the maintenance man. He cleaned up every night and fixed the things that were broken before they opened the next day. The windows were always shiny and clear. He loved working nights. He was a true night owl. Grandpa was a true renaissance man. He knew about everything and anything. He only had an eighth-grade education but had spent his whole life in search of knowledge. He taught himself to read sheet music at the age of 40. It wasn't that he couldn't play, he could. He played banjo and a guitar that could make you cry. He once sang in a car driving straight from Idaho Falls to L.A. without repeating a song. That's how many songs he knew. He'd even once been a hobo. I think that's where he learned a lot of the songs. When I lived with them, he was studying the dictionary. Yes, I said studying the dictionary. Why you ask? So, he could better work on his book of poetry. He was always writing poems, but he especially wanted to write alliterative poems and he needed to expand his vocabulary to accomplish his goal. He completed his work, and I even had the privilege of teaching his poetry to my literature class at a university when I was teaching. He was so proud and honored, but not as much as I was.

But above all these great things, Grandpa was a very deeply religious man. He had bounced between Mormonism, Bahai, and even Islam. So, when he found me crying at his kitchen table one day, he told me something that I never forgot. He asked, "Why are you crying?"

I said, "No one will ever love me." In my fountain of experience of two romantic relationships, I had been devastated. Both had not turned out the way I thought. One had moved on, literally, and the other turned out to be a liar and a thief. I had some physical issues too, and I thought life was over.

Grandpa said, "You know I'm a poet. We poets see things that other people don't see." At this point, I thought Grandpa had too much tea, but I listened respectfully. He continued, "I see you with a man with shoulders out to here (he stretched his arms as wide as they would go), and a waist down to here (he closed his arms in dramatic fashion to show a tiny waist in comparison to the shoulders), with a heart made of gold." Did I mention that he said tall, dark, and handsome as well? That's when I knew Grandpa was blowing smoke…come on. Where would I, the girl from a very small town in Utah, going to a slightly larger town in Utah, meet such a man? But I humored Grandpa and politely nodded my head.

So just imagine his face when he saw this tall, dark, handsome, man with shoulders walk through the door. Grandpa couldn't stop grinning. I couldn't stop grinning. Grandma couldn't stop cooking.

We had a great visit, and we drove all over—saw the frozen waterfalls that give their name to Idaho Falls, and even drove up to Jackson Hole, Wyoming. Driving on roads that have 10-foot-tall snow sides is not fun unless you are trying to drift—accidentally. I was okay with my tourist driving until we almost didn't make a very dark, very sharp left turn onto the freeway. To his credit, it wasn't properly marked, and he held it together rather well. I would find out throughout my life that when faced with sharp turns, and dark roads, he was the one, who you wanted at the wheel, trust me.

27 December 1982

It was still the Christmas break and there weren't many students around. I was alone and got a phone call to meet my 'tourist' in my dorm lobby. It was strange because it was 1:00 in the morning, but not unusual. I could tell by the look on his face he wanted to talk about something serious. I knew him that well already. He asked me to sit down. Now I was scared. We sat on the couch under the stairs. He said, "I've been given a choice." So far not earth-shaking.

I said, "What is the choice?"

He said, "I either have to go to South Dakota and study there with my cousin, or I have to marry you." Not the choice I was expecting. I was thinking along the lines of majors to study, and cars to buy, but not a life-changing decision. By now I was in tears as I had no idea what he wanted to do.

So, I blurted out, "So what do you want to do?"

He replied, "I want to be with you," without hesitation. My head was spinning...had he just said what I hoped, wanted, and wished he would say? Yes, he chose me.

"So exactly what does that mean?" I asked half sobbing.

"It means I want to marry you," he said. It wasn't the most romantic of proposals ever, but it was sincere. I hugged him and I cried. Of course, I want to be with you I thought. I had no idea what that meant, but at that moment, I didn't care. I'm sure he had no idea either, but we had each other. That was all that mattered. The next month was a blur of classes and thinking. What do we do now? Let's go to Disneyland.

January 1983

I hadn't been a big traveler. In fact, I had never been east of Evanston, Wyoming. I had been to L.A., but that was ages ago, so this trip was very special. My tourist and I were going to visit one of his best friends. I didn't know it, but there were many Palestinians coming to America. This one lived in Whittier, California. All I knew was it was close to Knotts berry Farm and Disneyland wasn't too far either. The friend was very gracious and took us all over L.A. At one point we ended up in Westwood (near UCLA) where there was a street fair/market. I had never seen anything like it. I would spend most of my adult life shopping from such places, but I didn't know that at the time.

There was one particular booth selling jewelry, and they had 14 kt gold rings. I had never liked diamonds, and still don't, and I knew we didn't have much money, so I picked a very plain gold band. 32$ seemed like a lot at the time. I didn't know I would spend the rest of my life accumulating gold pieces, but that gold band has always been my favorite.

On the way home, we stopped off in Las Vegas. We calculated how much we could spend on food and lodging, and most importantly gas money to get home. We had enough to get home, but not much left over. Certainly not enough to pay for even the cheapest of Vegas weddings. We knew when to hold them, and when to fold them. I opted to call my parents. That has to be one of the strangest phone calls ever. Mom asked, "Where are you?"

And I replied, "Las Vegas."

She then asked, "What are you doing in Las Vegas?"

To which I replied, "We just tried to get married, but we didn't have enough money." The line went silent, but I later found out she was telling my father what I had said.

His reply was priceless, "Well then I think you better bring him by the house on your way home. We need to meet this guy."

We did stop by the house, and they met him for the first time. Yes, he was Palestinian, and yes, he was Muslim. My mother gave me the obvious stare and question, "Why don't you wait to get married? There's no hurry is there?"

I replied, "No, we don't have to get married for obvious reasons, but for reasons of our own." My parents could never understand why we 'rushed' into getting married. After all, we had known each other for only three months, so what was the rush? The rush was that there was no such thing as 'dating' in Islam. If you were going out with someone, it had better be your fiancé. Nothing more nothing less. I was his fiancé and the sooner we got married, the sooner his tuition would drop by two-thirds. A bit pragmatic and romantic.

10 February 1983

A courthouse, a courtroom, a judge, and a flower. I wasn't religious, and there wasn't anyone in Ogden who could officially marry us in the Islamic tradition, so here we were, in front of a Justice of the Peace. I had my roommates; he had his roommate. It was all very civil—it was a civil marriage after all. But when the judge asked, "Do you Aiman Anwar Arafat take this woman to be your lawfully wedded wife?"

His answer was not what I expected. "Uh huh."

"Uh huh?" Are you kidding? Everyone knows you say, 'I do.'

I did the only thing I could and gave him a look that would melt steel, nudged him with my shoulder, and said, "You need to say, 'I do'." He did, and the judge said yada yada yada. I do not think either of us heard anything after I do. So, what romantic thing did we do after our 'I do's'? We went for pizza, of course.

May 1983

Of course, my parents knew we were married right away. They even threw us a wedding reception at a local motel a couple of months later. We hadn't wanted a reception, but as my mother reminded me, weddings and funerals weren't for the participants, they were for everyone else. My grandparents, parents, cousins, friends, roommates, and invited guests all showed up. The guests didn't show up till the unpredictable Utah weather did its famous four-seasons-in-one-day thing. We had a beautiful summer morning, followed by a springy afternoon, followed by high winds and a cold air-fallish feel, and then it really turned nasty and cold. It could have snowed if there had been any moisture in the air. But all that did was make sure that everyone who had been out in their garden preparing for the spring in the morning, came to our reception. My grandmother had made my dress. It was light blue, with puffy sleeves, and perfect. Aiman and his brother and even my brother were in the mandatory baby blue tuxes. Yes, we looked like something from the 1970s, but we had a great time seeing old family friends. I would wear it one more time, but that's told a bit later in the story.

His parents didn't find out until someone just happened to mention in passing that Aiman was married. The next time he called his parents after this, it was the first question. His mother started with, "Your third cousin, on your father's side, once removed, says that you are married. Is this true?"

My husband, being the very dutiful son that he was, couldn't lie, so he told the truth. "Yes, I am married to an American." I had no idea at the time, but she had actually fainted. I mean passed out cold. Of course, that was after she screamed like a banshee. The thought that her baby boy, the one that they had scraped and saved for so he could go to America, only to fall for the first bimbo that came along. The nerve of this girl. She wasn't even Muslim, was she?

I had been raised by a Mormon mother and a Catholic father from very rural southern Idaho. They shouldn't have even gotten married, let alone had children, at least according to their respective families. My paternal grandmother died when I was only six with my paternal grandfather going just a year before her, but I have such fond memories of them both. They say smell is the strongest memory trigger. Boy, can I attest to that? If I smell the right kind of tobacco or coffee, I'm right back in their house. I was the one relegated to the couch in the living room when we visited them. I had to listen to the cuckoo clock from Germany rings all night long. Obviously, I was fascinated by all the gears and levers and pull cords. What kid wouldn't be? But every time I got near it; someone would yell at me to stay clear. That would usually entail me running into a standing ashtray. They were everywhere. Remember what I said about tobacco smoke? If I smell tobacco and leather, all I can see is my grandfather's reclining chair. Not him, but the chair. He was always at work. It would take two heart attacks to take him though.

There was always a pot of coffee on the stove as well. You know back in the day, they would boil it till it was so bitter that it could peel paint off the walls? And they wouldn't waste the grounds used to make it either. They would dump them on all the flowerpots around the kitchen too. I wouldn't learn to appreciate coffee till I was well on my way to 40, but the smell always gets me.

To this day, I don't have a single plant in my house. Never have, probably never will. It's not that I don't like plants, I love them. It's that for the longest time I associated plants, flowers, and gardens with my paternal grandmother. She had row after row of African Violets on a shelf system in her kitchen that needed constant attention as there were so many and all required watering. These were her indoor plants of choice. They were everywhere. She had such a garden in her backyard filled with all kinds of flowers, growing up trellises, but I remember Irises the most. I never found out which came first, the need for the garden, or the need to get rid of all it produced. She was famous for her flower-arranging skills. She won prizes at the county and state fairs back when wheat arranging was still a skill. She never missed a wedding, baptism, or funeral for her local Catholic church.

I could spend hours out in her garden. She had a couple of statues in the garden just about my height at the time being around three years old and I would pretend and make up stories to entertain myself while the adults were playing cards. The only thing that was almost as holy as church, was playing Pinochle. This would be replaced with poker and an annual family poker tournament for fame and glory, but not money (long before everyone else on the planet discovered it). I have a vivid memory of interrupting the family card game and being shooed off upstairs until they were done in the wee hours of the morning to take up my space on the couch. Smoke and coffee. Maybe that's why I've stayed away from those two as well,

My parents had a Catholic wedding and a Mormon reception. That went over like a lead balloon. My paternal grandma wasn't well even before my parents married with the cancer that would eventually take her. But when I showed up seven months later, 'premature,' weighing in at 8 lbs., 6 oz in Provo, Utah, she would be my savior. She and my maternal grandmother would both save my life. But that's another story altogether. When you read about Adam, you'll get this part of my story. My little family would eventually end up on a newly purchased dairy farm in Orem, Utah.

Growing up on a farm has some rather unique opportunities; seeing animals being born, or rather pulled from their laboring mothers (calf pulling), rats the size of house cats, pigs digging up the baby fruit trees, playing Tarzan on the giant haystacks, but by far the best thing about growing up was my best friend who also lived on a dairy farm—Kathy.

She wasn't my best friend just because she had a Malibu Barbie and the pink car and the doll house to go with it, but because she played with me, and sang with me. She knew how to play the piano, and we would spend hours singing show tunes and playing with our dolls. Occasionally, we would play out in the corn fields behind her dad's milking barn. It could be wet, and muddy, and I would get my shoes stuck and then have to clean not only my shoes but my wet, sticky feet. Good times. You have no idea how much fun being scared to death playing hide and seek in a corn field can be. The absolute best thing was when we would fill up the small milking barn with water and pretend it was a swimming pool. Even if we didn't fill it up, it was still good for a water fight with the hoses that were there to spray off the cows before milking. When we got hungry, we would make sandwiches out of room-temperature butter, and then sprinkle sugar on them. Wonder bread never tasted so good.

I also had a giant front porch at my house that I used as my very own dance stage. I took dance lessons from an early age, and somewhere there are videos proving this. I was a lady bud, a grasshopper, and a fish. I would later use these dance skills to gain a part in a middle school musical where I tore up the stage in my fringe and ballet shoes. I would also have a part in the middle school musical that would be canceled because a boy accidentally blew himself up with a homemade pipe bomb. My teacher expected a lot out of a middle schooler when she wanted me to dance with a boy who was a class pariah. I did my best and upon reflection believe that that is where my respect and love of everyone came from. In high school, I tried out for the school dance team and was told that 'You can't be on the team because you can't be 'lifted' by a boy.'

Yes, I actually had a teacher tell me I was too fat to be a dancer, even though I was better than most. I never stopped dancing though. Remember the night I met my 'tourist'? I would go on to have many teachers and lessons: piano (where I would walk to it over a mile away and a scary highway to cross), clarinet that would turn into oboe lessons when I got braces (these were given at the local university by music college students). I even got to play my oboe for the town musical production of Carnival. It is very difficult to play an oboe and march in a marching band. So, what did the music teacher at my high school do? He switched me to cymbals when it was marching time. And when our high school marching band wanted to try something new, I was more than up for it—tall flags. We would toss and throw and catch those six-foot-long poles. It took hours and hours to get synchronous and even more hours to get synchronous with the band. But I was good at most everything I tried. At least I tried.

It was also scary growing up on a farm. Machines all over that you weren't supposed to touch, cars driving in the driveway at all speeds, your own dog that bit you, but didn't leave you afraid of dogs, untamed bulls that gored your uncle and put him in the hospital, a wild dog that tore up the house and then you got your own room. Dad was afraid that this wild dog, which had wandered onto our property, would hurt either our own dogs or some of the animals, so he locked it in the house for the day while he ran around. Bad idea. The dog tore the living room curtains to shreds, along with most of the cushions on the couches. He also destroyed most of the curtains in the bedrooms as well. The good thing to come out of this was that not only did I get my dream bedroom set from Sears (the canopy bed in blue), but I also got my own room. Bad dogs weren't the only harm on the farm, being thrown from a horse while riding at full speed, isn't fun. It is also a good thing a tetanus shot lasts five to ten years…stepping on nails, rakes, and other farm implements can leave holes in not just your shoes, but your feet as well. You get the idea.

But it wasn't just the farm that was dangerous. Cars/trucks can be just as dangerous. One day, my very young baby brother and I accompanied my father to visit a fellow farmer. I vividly remember trying to open my door but having to give up the attempt. I climbed out my father's door. This would prove to be an almost fatal mistake on my part. When the visit was finished, we piled into the truck through the same door we all climbed out of. On our way back to our house, which couldn't have been more than two miles away, my father made a left turn. A turn that he had made hundreds of times. But because I had partially opened the door, not realizing it at the time, of course, it flew open on me. Being the dutiful older sister that I was, I put my left hand out on my brother, and would you believe I thought I could reach and just pull the door shut? Ok, the brain of a six-year-old isn't an adult brain.

What actually happened was that gravity and momentum worked together to pull me out of the truck. I went flying, and then skidding on the road. My father swore until his last day that he believed he had run me over with the dual back wheels on his Chevy truck. Again, inertia was in my favor. I kept going and rolled out of the way of the wheels. Undeniably, when a moving object hits a non-moving object, something has to give way and the road wasn't giving way. I believe because of all the raw milk I had drunk as a child; I didn't break a bone. I hit the pavement so hard that I was picking gravel out of my knees and elbows weeks later. But that was all. Two skinned knees, two skinned elbows, and a raw chin. I remember hearing the squeal of the wheels and smelling the smoke as Dad hit the brakes. He was overjoyed to hear me crying. Remember he thought he had run me over! The noise from the brakes was so loud that the lady in the corner house came running out to see what had happened! My dad didn't know whether to laugh or cry at the moment. He scooped me up in his big arms and laid me down on the seat of the truck. The next thing I remember is running into the house squealing like a stuck pig and my mother saying, "What happened?"

All I could squeak out was, "I fell out of the truck." I started first grade with two scraped knees and two scraped elbows. I looked a mess, but no one messed with me either.

On the same note that vehicles can be dangerous, my father is the only person I know to have run over himself. Yes, you read correctly, he actually ran himself over with a tractor. How is that possible you ask? This is a farm, so we had a tractor. It was a bit temperamental, meaning it would start or not or run or not. Let's put it this way, Dad was not a handy man. If it couldn't be fixed with bailing wire or duct tape, it couldn't be fixed. So, one Sunday morning, my father needed the tractor for something and tried to wake my mother up to help him. Because it was Sunday, it was her day to sleep in and she didn't get up right away. When she did, she got to the kitchen window to check on my father. His idea was to pull the tractor to the top of a short hill with his truck, then unhitch the tractor and let it roll down the short hill and jump on and pop the clutch to start it. Mom was watching as he jumped out of the truck, unhitched the tractor, got it rolling down hill, but then missed the step to get on the tractor and proceeded to get hit in the head by the manure scraper on the back of the tractor. Needless to say, the tractor stopped a short distance away. Mom thought he had been run over by the big back wheel, but it had just missed him. He was very lucky.

Changing one farm for another when I was 12 wasn't the defining moment I thought it would be. Nor was moving from one small town to an even smaller town going to change much either. I changed one click group for another. Moving only made me stronger, and more determined to define my own world. I would never be accused of being a follower. I tried out for the high school drama plays and got the lead parts in the plays: Blythe Spirit and Arsenic and Old Lace. One night when the lead male character was supposed to come down the stairs (our drama teacher was a whiz at creating sets by the way), he got a nosebleed while waiting up there and used his tie to help stop the bleeding. But that wasn't when I lost it. It was when I answered the door to let people in during Arsenic and Old Lace and the door fell to the floor. We all lost it for a minute laughing but tried to carry on as if that was quite normal to have the door fall into the room and not swing open.

I loved drama class. It was where I felt I fit in. I fit in with all the other misfits. I was in the marching band, the drama club, and the vocational education class, but not the dance group. None of these circles overlapped except for me. I hung out with a group of girls that would never make the most popular list; in fact, my mother even questioned me one time, "Why do you hang out with those loser girls? They aren't going to amount to anything in life?"

I completely forgot my answer to her, but she would never forget what I replied, "It's better than eating alone at lunchtime." We never spoke about my choice of friends again. For my senior year in high school, we got time to drive to a local elementary school to be a T.A. for an elementary teacher in the vocational child care class. To this day I have no idea why no one would ride with me in my hand-me-down Chevy half-ton truck. I loved that truck. It was the truck I learned to drive in. It was a four-wheel drive with a four-speed gear shift. Just because it smelled like horse shit, what was their problem? My father had gotten a new truck but hadn't sold this one yet, and it was drivable. At 16, anything with an engine and wheels that moves will be taken.

My favorite memory of that truck is my one and only driving lesson from my father. It was a fall day in Utah, which meant it could rain, snow, sleet, or all at the same time at any time. My father called me from my room and said, "You're driving me to Payson." Payson was two towns south on the freeway from where we lived. It had started to rain, I was nervous enough, but wanted to show I could do this. Shifting was ok but trying to hold a stick shift on a hill, and waiting for traffic signals, on slick roads, was my idea of a nightmare. I survived, but barely. That was the parenting style I grew up with.

I was raised in a home where I only saw my parents argue once in my life. I mean a real doozy. And indubitably, it was about me, and about religion. Remember, Dad had been raised Catholic, and Mom had been raised Mormon, but both had left religion a long time ago. I was 14. I was at a crossroads in my life. Or rather Dad was under pressure because we weren't paying tithing and I was getting all the benefits from the church. I either had to become a full member of the Mormon Church or quit going. At least that's what my father said. That's what started the argument. My mother thought I should wait until I was old enough to make my own decisions. According to Mormon teachings, I was way old enough, eight being the age of baptism, but according to my mother, I needed to grow up just a bit more, but my father wasn't going to allow me to wait.

Consequently, at 14, I was given an ultimatum. Did I want to be baptized into the Mormon Church or not? I had been 'active' in all the social events since I could remember. I was very active in the Mormon girls' groups. I had even memorized some of their holy book passages. Before I made this momentous decision, my mother wanted me to read something. I was an avid reader, so no problem. It was the Tanner's book, *Mormonism: Shadow or Reality.* Remember this is long before the internet. This was when fax machines were high-tech. It was a very thick book, but that was because it was a photocopy of a photocopy. By the time I was about a quarter of the way through, I was convinced that

I didn't want to belong to the church. I didn't want to belong to any church. My grandfather would be a bit disappointed, but he knew how my mother had thrown the baby out with the bath water when it came to religion, so he wasn't surprised by my decision. It was my decision after all. One that I didn't regret at all until I met my Muslim man.

So, when I wanted to marry the most incredible man on the planet, my 'tourist' proceeded to tell me that first, he couldn't marry me as I was. What? After all, we had just been through with his decision to stay in Utah, and now he tells me he can't marry me. Huh? He went on to explain that if I were Mormon, Catholic, or even Jewish he could marry me no problem, as these are the people of the book. But because I didn't have a religion, I wasn't a 'person of the book' and he couldn't marry me. So, what was the solution? Exactly what my father had done 20 years before. I converted for love. I said the Shahada. I was aware of the words, but not the connotation of the words. That revelation would come much later and only after much searching and questioning everything I had been taught to believe or not believe as it were.

In answer to his mother's question, yes, I was Muslim. Many of the young Arabs living and studying in America at the time were getting married for a 'green card.' I was getting married for a 'paradise card.' Actually, that was why his mother had fainted. She had been hearing everything about the loose American women and was terrified that her son was marrying 'one of those girls.' Not a nice home girl who knew how to cook and clean and raise proper Muslim children. I hated to cook, and cleaning was worse. I adored children though.

February 1983

For the next year, we lived in a tiny little house in the middle of town. We spent our wedding night sleeping on the floor because we hadn't bought a bed yet. A bit later, we received as a wedding gift, my bed, that Sears canopy bed, that I grew up sleeping on. It was a double, so we fit snugly, but well. Did I mention that our little house was under some rather large sycamore trees with a front yard and a backyard? It was lovely to go outside and sit in the front yard. It wasn't so lovely when a huge windstorm came along one fall evening and blew one of those trees onto our bedroom! The landlord repaired the roof, but we couldn't afford to stay there. We were two poor college students who couldn't afford even a small house. We moved to a single-room apartment that was closer to the college.

March 1984

Life wasn't exactly going as expected. I had lost my job, and the best Aiman could find without a degree was as a cashier at the college during events such as basketball games, etc. It meant that we went to all the basketball games, but we didn't get to watch much. Somehow, we managed to scrape together enough money to buy two round-trip tickets to fly to see his parents in Gaza. It was about time; we'd been married a whole year and his family had never even met me.

I had never been east of Evanston, Wyoming, and now I was going to fly halfway around the world. In fact, I looked at a scaled globe in the library and ran my finger over the top from Utah and down to Gaza. It wasn't a finger width more or less. The time difference was 11 hours. It was halfway around the world. I'm a bit claustrophobic, but the excitement and thrill won the day. We flew TWA from Salt Lake to Denver, Denver to New York, New York to Paris, and Paris to Tel Aviv. I remember catching a glimpse of the Statue of Liberty out the plane window. That was all I got though. We had connecting flights, and not much time to make them. At Charles de Gaulle Airport, I was shocked to find a restroom attendant who not only was standing there watching you but insisted on being paid to do so. I slept a lot and dreamed a lot.

I was scared, nervous, happy, excited, anxious, but above all, happy. I was happy to be going somewhere, anywhere. I wasn't the 'most likely to go nowhere' girl anymore. I was out of my one-horse town for good.

When we landed at Ben Gurion Airport in the middle of the night, I was mentally and physically exhausted, but the fun was just beginning. First, we were singled out of the incoming passengers because I held an American passport, and my husband had flown on a U.S. re-entry permit. Yes, you read correctly. He only had a document that would let him re-enter the United States. He had an Israeli ID, but he didn't want to use it unless he had to. He didn't have to. But that didn't save us from Israeli immigration and border patrol though. They insisted on going through every item that we had brought with us. That wouldn't have been so bad if it had been done in a room, behind closed doors. It was done out in the open, with my tighty-whities on display for the entire world to see.

You must remember that this was 1984. Gaza had been occupied by the Israeli forces since 1967, and they had been acting as the de-facto government ever since. They were in charge of the schools, the hospitals, the roads, the sanitation, everything. Of course, that meant that if something was done, it was done at a glacial speed and with as much red tape as possible.

They were thorough in their search and found a small tie pin with a map of Palestine in the inside pocket of his suit jacket. Oh no. No one was allowed any flag, map, or reference to Palestine in Palestine. It was as if it didn't exist. They didn't want it to exist. Damn. What were we going to do now? A security guard asked, "Do you have any other contraband?"

My husband looked him in the eye and said, "I wish I did, but no, that is all I brought." I'm sure they didn't believe him, but because he had admitted that he wished he'd had more, maybe they did believe him.

When they were finished rummaging through our entire luggage, we were left to put it all back in. If you have ever traveled, you know it never fits in again the way it did the first time. Somehow, we managed to get everything back in.

By now, it was the darkest time of night. The lights had an orange glow from the incandescent bulbs. Everything was either black or orange. I was trying to see everything at once. I wanted to be able to recall everything I was seeing. I was on sensory overload. I must have fallen asleep somewhere between the airport and the Erez checkpoint. It was a trailer. This was the border. A trailer? Quite a letdown.

We went by a Seba Raqib. A Seba Raquib is a seven-passenger Mercedes Benz limousine. However, when I say limo, it doesn't mean quite the same as in the west. There were no T.V. monitors, no champagne bowls, actually no nothing. It was quite sparse and actually quite uncomfortable to sit in the middle row of seats. It was much better to sit in the front seat or the back row. Nevertheless, that meant you had to be one of the first people to request that car. And it was always a first come first served proposition. More than once, we opted for another car rather than sit in the middle. But for this trip, I would have sat on the roof if I had to. The strange orange glow from the streetlights was something I never really got used to but learned to accept as the signal that we were almost home.

It may have been getting on toward dawn, but everything was a dull brown. I would later learn that it is a fine dust that coats everything. Even the trees were this dull brown color because it hardly rains most of the year. And I couldn't see the houses except for the parts that were taller than the walls. There were walls around every house. I grew up in open spaces where the only barrier was a fence that you could crawl through or over. Here, every plot of land was surrounded by at least a six-foot-high wall of bricks. Bouncing down the dusty road I could only imagine what the cement houses looked like behind these walls.

I could smell the orange trees. I grew up in the west, in a high desert. We had apple, cherry, and peach trees, but not oranges. Nothing prepares you for the smell of orange from an orange plantation. Gaza has been famous for its oranges for tens of years. During the good years, they exported tons to other places throughout the Middle East. During the bad times, these orchards were bombed or bulldozed at random. There are a few of these plantations left, but not many. Most of the land has been converted to much-needed housing to accommodate the exploding population that can't leave.

We pulled up to one of those high walls and stopped. This was it. Really? A dusty street, full of dusty walls, with dusty two-story houses behind them, surrounded by dusty palm trees. Definitely not the stuff of postcards. I would learn later that this was actually a 'newer' home. The old style of home was built more on the Turkish style of a courtyard surrounded by rooms of one story or two. A very good friend would move into one of those much later. She said it was very strange to open the door and suddenly find yourself out in the open. If you wanted to visit the kitchen, you would walk across the courtyard. Eating was done out in the open unless it was raining. Then it all moved indoors to another room.

Our house was a complete house with rooms inside and a huge backyard. My husband loved to describe all the trees and plants he grew there as a child. They were mostly gone now. Not cared for and trampled underfoot by so many people who didn't have the love and care for the earth as he did.

I thought the stairs would never end. I was tired and jet-lagged as it was. It was such a shiny surface, and the railing/wall was so pristine. I would later learn that it had been painted in my honor. There were a lot of things done in my honor.

I had, of course, tried to prepare myself for his large family, but to put names to faces was the only way to handle it. I had had no experience with twins, so I wasn't prepared for the shock of my life…they weren't kidding when they said identical. It would take a couple of weeks for me to figure out which one of his youngest brothers was Eyad, and which was Anees. That left all the others…Ashraf, Amjad,

Islam, Ehab, and his only sister, Eman. Thank God he had only one sister…I could remember her name, right? When you don't have a reference for names it makes them twice as hard to remember. But the siblings weren't the only ones I met that day…I met the whole family downstairs—Uncle Sami, Aunt Fadua, cousins Badera, Sereen, Suha, and Samir. Now how was I supposed to remember all these names instantly? They had had a lifetime to remember them. I did my best and used 'you' a lot.

The house on the second floor was rather large, but that was because it was originally two apartments, not one big house. My husband's uncle lived there until 1967 and then left for Kuwait. My husband's family didn't try to occupy the other half for years until it was established that they weren't coming back any time soon, and the family was growing so they needed the room. They literally knocked a hole in the wall that had separated the two houses, so to get to the other side; you had to walk through a little hole. It would become a full-blown door while I visited. Remember I said they had done a lot in my honor?

We stayed with his family for three months. I remember getting up and eating with the whole family every day—there was so much food, and it was usually gone so fast. There was cheese—at least three kinds (feta, cheddar, Emmental), olives—at least two kinds (black and green—of which they had cracked and pickled) or more, a pan of scrambled eggs, duga, zatar (ground up thyme with sesame seeds and olive oil mixed), olive oil, occasionally fool and/or falafel, and, of course, fresh Arabic bread, jam, or honey when the salty items were finished. Did I mention the fresh bread? His mother would whip up a batch of dough, proof it throughout the day, and then spend the evening cooking it in the living room, in the oven in the hallway, or both.

The hallway had a propane cylinder, but the gadget in the living room was electric. She would place a piece of dough on the top of the electric pan, and then once it cooked a bit, she would then place it under the element to cook the other side. It was quite the process, and she did fifty pieces at a time. She had a house full of young growing boys—need I say more? Yes, my brothers-in-law were approximately, 17, 13, 11, and 7, and the twins were only 6. There is no taste on earth quite like freshly baked bread. I remembered the dinner rolls my grandmother used to make for Thanksgiving…they were to die for. We would eat those till we almost burst. Remember that one year, I thought for sure my brother would. He ate so much turkey dinner that he rolled on the floor for two hours in pain. Grandma knew how to do a turkey. She would have been so proud of my reputation for making a roast turkey dinner, but I got ahead of myself. Back to the bread.

Americans eat meat three times a day; Palestinians eat bread three times a day. We used it to eat breakfast as seen above, and for lunch, which was usually the largest of the day, and for a late dinner that looked a lot like breakfast.

After I had been introduced to the entire family and had barely unpacked my suitcases, we were all invited downstairs to the uncles for a welcome lunch. I had been told that this was a tradition and that they had spared no expense or time in preparing for this meal. It was to become one of the most memorable meals of my life. The main course was 'qarash.' Qarash is stuffed beef or lamb intestines. Even though I had grown up on a farm and seen my share of farm life; including sheep being born, cows artificially inseminated, pigs slaughtered as well as chickens having their heads cut off, nothing prepared me for this. Being the guest, I was offered the stomach. Believe me when I say, my stomach almost made an appearance that day. I tried ever so graciously to decline their offer of any of it. Then it took a turn for the worse if you can believe that.

Someone stirred the pot of green slime, which I later learned was a local delicacy named 'molokia.' In English, it's called 'Jews mallow' and is supposed to have been the food of the kings and queens of Egypt. As far as I could see, the kings and queens could keep it. Then suddenly there were eyes staring up at me from the green slime! And to my horror, teeth! Yes, you read right, teeth. They had killed a rabbit and put the head and all in the molokia—to give it flavor! It was everything I could do to keep from losing my lunch—literally! I learned how to politely say no in Arabic, very quickly. This was only the first of many faux pas' I would commit over the next three months. I managed to get through the lunch with my lunch intact, but I still don't know how. Lots and lots of fresh bread—plain thank you.

Gold Souk

In getting ready for the big day—my coming out party as it were, I was taken to the old gold market in the heart of downtown Gaza. Driving there, I was again assaulted by the dull gray color of everything. We drove past hundreds of years old walls, just left to fall down of their own weight. At one point, there was a tree in the middle of the road. Yes, I said middle of the road. They hadn't chopped it down, just built the road to go around it. It became a sort of 'round about.' Then on to the gold market at the top of the hill that is the 'old part of Gaza.' Try to imagine a thousand-year-old domed roof covered with soot and dirt from the centuries and seemed out of a Hollywood movie set. Now make that older, dustier, and mustier, and you have the gold market.

It was actually quite narrow, and only about a block and a half long, but if the walls could talk—what stories of love, and sorrow would they tell? People didn't only go there to buy, but they sold as well. If you had a unique and good-condition piece, it might avoid the scrap pile. Otherwise, it would be broken and melted down to make the next item of jewelry to be worn by a new bride. Gaza was famous for its wide and thick bracelets. They had been the style for more than a hundred years. They were easy to make—roll out a thick bracelet, and then with just a little work they 'stamped' it with a bevel as intricate and delicate work had been reserved for Italy, India, or now Bahrain.

When I saw it, I knew it was mine. It was wide and nearly half an inch across solid gold. I have always preferred gold to any other metal, and especially more than silver. I have a few silver pieces, but mostly I am in love with the yellow metal that never tarnishes, or rusts. In taking me to the gold market, the family was continuing a tradition that is as old as time—a bride price. Most people misunderstand and confuse this with a dowry. A dowry is what a woman is expected to pay to a man and his family to marry her. This is mostly applied in India and the subcontinent, and would you believe Egypt? A bride price is the money (or guarantee of goods or a house) that a man pays to the woman's family in order to marry her. Most women use this money to buy gold and use a little of the money to buy clothing, makeup, or even furniture for the new house, etc.

What I didn't know at the time was that most women buy a complete set of gold…earrings, bracelet, ring, and necklace—all matching. I was under the impression that I could get just one item, and if that was the case, I was going to pick the biggest piece I could find, not a measly little ring or smaller earrings. I have since seen bracelets that cover from the wrist to the elbow and trust me when I say if I had seen that I would have bought it at that time.

To get into the shops, you had to go down a slope because the road had been built up over the centuries and the market was on the level of the ancient original streets. The doors were so small that only one person could enter at a time, and their safes had been knocked into little niches in the walls. The lighting wasn't as sophisticated as a mall or jewelry store, but who cared when the light was bouncing off all that liquid yellow? I had never seen anything so assaulting on the eyes before in my life. Everywhere you turned, there was a waterfall of metal that ended in a spectacular pool of metallic circles. It literally took my breath away. I couldn't imagine there was that much gold in the whole world, let alone just hanging in windows. Much later in my life, I would remember this feeling as I was walking down the corridors of the gold market in Dubai and marveling at the hundreds of shops with liquid yellow in the windows. They say gold is rare and that's why it's expensive. Rare my foot.

A Spring Day in 1984

The preparations for this day had taken 19 years. Yes, you read correctly, 19 years! My mother-in-law had been preparing for this day since my husband had been born. He was her oldest child, and he was her son. Mothers take their filial duty to get their boys married to a suitable girl. What is a suitable girl? A girl from a good family—reputation is everything, a girl who has been educated, a girl who knows how to keep her son in the style he has become accustomed to—by cooking his favorite dishes and cleaning the house every day. I, of course, didn't fit any of that. I don't like to cook and certainly didn't know how to make any Palestinian dishes. I hated cleaning more than I hated cooking. And I was definitely not from a 'good' family. Most people had only heard about American girls from the boys who came back and married a 'nice girl' after having sowed their oats in America. I did my best to allay their fears, but language was proving a difficult mountain to overcome.

I had brought my grandmother-made wedding dress. That seemed to impress them, but more that I had a grandmother than that she had made it. The actual preparations for this day took only a couple of days. The cleaning and moving of various metal and plant-made structures made way for them to build a stage. And I do mean a stage: complete with backdrop and everything. I had done some acting in high school but trust me when I say nothing prepared me for 250 women and children all trying to eat me in their eyes! I was the main attraction and I think they would have paid to see me. I was the exotic wild creature from across the sea. Of course, once they saw that I really didn't have two heads, nor was I dressed like a burlesque show, they calmed down and the real party started.

I fancied myself as a dancer at one point, you will remember the high school teacher, but all those years of training didn't prepare me for Arabic belly dancing. They did, however, train me to follow and pick up moves quickly. Thank God, I had had those lessons. It paid off big time. I was able to watch ladies move, and then emulate what they were doing. I wasn't half bad, and the crowd went wild. Did I mention that in order to show your hips, they tie a scarf around your waist? They leave nothing to chance; they want to see it all. No faking in this dance. Either you've got rhythm, or you don't. I didn't have the moves exactly, but I had the beat. I watched as my new sister-in-law danced, my mother-in-law danced, hell, half the neighborhood danced. How did they know how to do that?

There was something that sounded like a banshee cry and nearly scared the socks right off me, but I would learn later that it was very traditional, and that it was really poking fun at the newlyweds and family. I came to appreciate how hard it is to make the traditional ululation after trying it a couple of times. It takes years of practice to get it right, but when they do, it carries for a long way. This was all new to me but felt very primal and I wasn't intimidated. I got up and showed the crowd that a girl from a small-town USA knew a thing or two about moving to music. I would come to love the sound and rhythm of a singer called Abdul Wahab. Most Arabs find his music to be too old-fashioned, but I love his music. I don't understand a word of what he is singing about, but his deep throaty voice reminds me of my guitar-playing and banjo-picking grandfather.

For me, the most interesting part was the passing of drinks. There wasn't any wedding cake or tables or reception line. There was a mass of people sitting all bunched as close to the stage as possible. They have managed to turn a wedding party into a full-on contact sport, but back to the drinks. So, my brother-in-law showed up with crates of small bottles of cola and sprite looking drinks. It was one mad rush to pass as many bottles as quickly as possible. Some women were stuffing them into their purses, little children were crying because their mothers couldn't open them fast enough. It was organized chaos. All I could do was flash back to when I was very small and driving around with my father as he traveled around rural Utah. I remember stopping at gas stations and grabbing a bottle of coke out of a machine. The only problem with that was that you had to drink it quickly because you needed to give the gas station back the bottle. It was difficult for a small girl to drink a whole bottle.

Thank God, the glass was thick because, of course, children were dropping bottles right and left. I was the dish de jour. Everyone couldn't get close enough or stare enough at me. It takes a pretty thick skin to be able to have that many people devour you with their eyes. I have no idea how models or actresses do this every day. Not my idea of a good time.

They weren't playing Abdul Wahab at the wedding festival. They were playing all the latest singers and songs at the time. At a wedding party, the music needs to be louder than what the human ear can handle, at least that's my perception of it. Every party I attended after this was like that. You had to scream at the person you wanted to talk to.

Every once in a while, the music would stop, and people would be caught shouting at one another. It made for humorous moments during a very festive time. And it always felt very festive at these wedding parties. Unlike all the receptions I had attended growing up, very formal and proscribed, these parties felt more like a sporting match—who could get the closest to the stage without actually being on the stage. You showed up two hours early, stayed until they passed out drinks, and then left.

For my party, I didn't even get to pass out 'Im labass.' This was a small porcelain gift you gave wrapped in plastic with Jordan almonds and the invitation to the party. I would collect tens of these over the years, with a corner stand overflowing with them. Each had a story attached, but I didn't do one as my party was planned in such haste, just like my gold, I had no idea until much later what the protocol was.

May 1984

I can't take it anymore. It is either her or me. My perfect marriage was falling apart at the seams. I gave my husband an ultimatum: her or me. The her was his mother, of course. When you ruin the plans of 19 years, you start on the wrong foot. It never really recovered, even after I charmed the neighborhood with my dancing. Ok, I threw a wrench in the works when I complained about her to an American girl I met, who promptly went to her husband and blabbed all that I said in confidence. Little did she know, or I, that he only married her for the green card, and in reality, he didn't love her, and in fact talked bad about her behind her back, but I digress. He told my story to his mother who was my mother-in-law's mother's neighbor, and they were only too happy to tell tales about me thinking that my husband had married me only for the green card too. So, the next time we went over to my husband's grandparent's house, the proverbial you know what hit the fan.

How could I disgrace the whole family by spreading news about my mother-in-law, and to a total stranger? Would you believe my mother-in-law's mother actually defended me? She reminded me so much of my own maternal grandmother—four feet tall, by four feet wide. They could have been twins. She defended me by saying how difficult it must be for me to have her as my mother-in-law. How she had treated me as her own mother-in-law had treated her; not fairly. I believe that the terrible mother-in-law jokes were made by Middle Eastern people to describe how they feel about them.

It is true; I was very young and very naïve about the world, but sometimes you have to stick up for yourself, and I wasn't a wilting violet when it came to what I wanted or felt I deserved. It got so bad that his father even went to the travel agent to change my ticket. If I left him and went back, then that was then end of our short marriage. Even with that ultimatum, I was sticking to my guns.

We stayed up all night talking. I couldn't tell you the conversation, but in the end, I agreed to loosen up and not put so much pressure on him, and he agreed to talk to his mother and explain that against all her wishes; she wasn't the top female in his life anymore. We would both have to compromise, neither of us was overly thrilled, but at least I was staying.

And if you're going to be staying, why not stick up for family? That's what family does—sticks up for one another. Remember there was the Israeli army patrolling the streets all over Gaza City, and on one particular day, this would prove fateful for all those involved. My brothers-in-law were in the shop around the corner from the family house like a normal day. My mother-in-law was always stopping by whenever she could just to make sure they were keeping up the standards of the family business. For some reason, I was alone with her in the shop when two soldiers came marching in and demanded that my brother-in-law go with them to be questioned just like that—no reason, no cause, just because they could. My brother-in-law had a knife that he cut the kunafa with in his hand, and he raised it to fend off the attack.

My mother-in-law jumped in front of one of the soldiers only to be butted in her head by an M-16 rifle. She had to have been in her mid-50s at the time, and they knew it. When she got hit, I, of course, ran over to help her and for my trouble got butted by the end of the same rifle. The soldiers wouldn't leave and by now were brandishing those M-16s in everyone's faces. I had seen a U.N. car pull up full of two U.N. 'soldiers.' I ran across the road to beg for their help. I explained what was going on and to my absolute shock and horror, they told me they could only 'report' what they saw as they had no authority to take any action even for a U.S. citizen who had been threatened and hit by the soldiers. They promised to write a report later. A lot of good that does anyone, just ask Rachel Corrie. She was an unarmed protester when she was killed by an Israeli armored bulldozer that ran her over! This was one of many times my brother-in-law would be arrested.

June 1984

Why does food taste better with sand between your toes? I have yet to figure that one out. But it always strikes me as quite funny, that it is so true. With a property that is mostly sand, what can you do? You can plant all kinds of trees and bushes and let the children run around. So, that's what they did. We ate barbecued chicken and rice, and for dessert, we had kunafa. I haven't mentioned this before, have I?

My husband's grandfather and his older brother were apprentice bakers for a Lebanese baker back in 1910ish. They learned how to make all kinds of sweets, including the Arabic sweet known as kunafa. They opened their own little shop, with their mother helping, in the heart of downtown Gaza in 1912, near the gold souk, where the family still owns the building, but not before spending time seasonally in Beersheba in the Negev desert. They had a cafeteria/tent where they would serve food to the Turkish soldiers and if they paid, it was fine; if they didn't, that was fine too. This was WWI. Did soldiers carry cash? I have no idea, but they made enough to make it worth their while. Enough so that they could open up that bakery.

How to describe kunafa? Think of cake meets a crunchy brownie and they had a child—kunafa. It is floury, crunchy, nutty, sticky, and above all, sweet. It actually is a very labor-intensive process, but the final product can't be beat. It also can't be made by machine as the final stage involves browning to just the right color. If you leave it too long, it's burned, if you take it off too soon, it's not crunchy, but soggy. It takes a real master to make it. If you want real exotic, you order it with a stretchy cheese like mozzarella or akawi cheese.

My father-in-law was a student at the university in his last year when his own father died suddenly. The bakery didn't have anyone to take over as his uncle wasn't able to do the hard labor, he was the cashier, and all the other seven brothers were either too young or were abroad studying at university. Who would be able to fill the shoes, and take care of the family? My father-in-law stepped up and never completed university—but he helped put all of his siblings through school. This meant that he accidentally inherited the family business—kunafa making. He was so good at it that he could tell just by testing the sugar water between his fingers if it needed more sugar or more water. It was a very tough and taxing life, but it supported not only his siblings but his own family when they came along. By then, he had bought out his uncle and cousin and owned the business outright.

I can still see the three-foot round steel pan full of kunafa. It wasn't the cheese kind either, but the one filled with walnuts. I wasn't a big fan of this kind, but on this day, what can I say, the sand between my toes had a strange effect. Ok, maybe not the sand so much as the announcement that I was pregnant. I remember eating half the pan—literally.

We had made up and thought it a good idea to go to a wedding that was going to be held in the Nile Hilton. I had never been to Egypt and the thought of seeing the pyramids made me weak in the knees. I had my American passport, and he had…a re-entry permit. What could go wrong?

This was the first time we had ever tried to cross to Egypt, and it wouldn't be the last. Nor would it be the first or last time that my husband would go to the Israelis to get permission to leave his own country. We knew the wedding was coming up, and we sought to get permission a couple of weeks in advance. He would go every day to the compound only to be told to come back the next day. He kept trying and the day of the wedding arrived.

He went to the compound as usual but insisted on seeing the person in charge. Once they figured out that he wasn't leaving until he got the aforementioned permission, they ushered him into an office. He explained that today was the wedding and if we didn't leave now, we wouldn't need to leave at all. The soldier listened and noticed that my husband had said 'we.' He then proceeded to ask about my name and why he wasn't asking for my permission. My husband told him that I was American. This was when being American still held some sway. He commented, "Oh," and promptly opened the drawer in his desk, shuffled some passports, found my husband's, and handed it over. The stamp on the paper that would allow him to leave had been dated for the day after we turned it in! It had been sitting on this man's desk for two weeks. Great. Now we could leave. This was about 1:00 in the afternoon. The border didn't close until 5:00. We still had time…maybe.

We had to take a special taxi just to get us to the border in time. By the time we got to Khan Younis, and I saw the (Cyprus) trees in the middle of the road, I was dumbfounded. They had built the road around those giant trees. They were incredible. The bark was that creamy white like in the story of the silver trees. They weren't evergreens, but I never saw them without leaves either. The branches hung over the road like an umbrella. The border crossing was unlike anything I had heard about, let alone lived through. We were shuffled into a hall where the passports would be stamped. We paid the fee to leave and then were herded onto a non-air-conditioned bus (remember this is June, in the desert!) where we waited until the Israelis were ready to let us cross. We rode for about three minutes, yes you read correctly, a three-minute ride that was as expensive as a full day pass at Disney Land.

Not being familiar with how we would be treated on the other side, I was totally unprepared for what happened next. Even before the Egyptians would stamp our passports, we had to exchange around 200$ for each person with a terrible exchange rate (25% lower than outside) into Egyptian pounds. The exchange rate at the border is laughable, but it was required, and we had to do it, so we did. It had taken the better part of a whole day to get here, but we made it in time. Or so we thought. We then proceeded to get our passports stamped. We were told to wait, and they would call our names. When they finally called our names, we were told he wasn't being allowed into the country, but I could go without him. We protested, we argued, we cried. All to no avail.

Ok, so he wasn't going to be let in, even though he held an Egyptian travel document that was issued to Palestinians. That wasn't the problem. The problem came when we wanted our exchanged money back. We were never going to find the rate they had charged us, and we were going to lose a lot. Remember, we were starving college students and we couldn't lose any amount of money, let alone a lot. Then we were told the 'bank' was closed for the day. The bank man had gone home, so they would have to call him back by walkie-talkie. When my husband refused to leave until someone opened up the bank and gave us back our money, we found ourselves surrounded by eight rather large border guards. He didn't back down. He said, "You're going to have to carry me out of here, but I'm not leaving without my money." And he meant it.

What scared me was how quickly we had gone from a nice trip to a wedding to almost being beaten and arrested in a foreign country. The same people had earlier stopped and beaten up and thrown out a young college boy. He was sent back. We thought that was going to happen to us. Eventually, once they understood he meant what he said, and I kept yelling in American English that I wasn't leaving, they found the man who could 'open the bank' for us. He finally showed up, but only after a big shot had heard our yelling and commotion, we got our money back, but by this time, we had missed the last bus across the border. We couldn't get in and we couldn't get out. Guess where we slept? The floor of the border mosque. It was the only floor that I trusted to be semi-clean. I can't describe how gross, filthy, smelly, and disgusting the bathroom there was. How human females managed to get urine and feces everywhere, but in the toilet is beyond me. They had closed the terminal, and the mosque was the only place we could go. Needless to say, that wasn't a night I have ever forgotten. We 'woke up' the next day to drive all the way home. I wouldn't make it to Egypt for another ten years. But it was worth the wait.

Jerusalem 1984

In reality, Jerusalem is only 60 miles from Gaza. But it might as well have been the moon for most of the people living in the Gaza Strip. How can I possibly describe one of the oldest cities in the world? To see the walls of the old city for the first time was, to say the least, breathtaking. They were a creamy white that's called locally, Jerusalem stone. They were tall, to be sure, but after driving through a crowded city to see the walls that had seen millennia of fighting and wars and life, I just couldn't believe I was actually there. To see the ramparts and killing holes was to see living history. But before even stepping foot close to the walls, I would taste the old city. We had to stop for the traditional bread 'Kaik.' This was a round rectangular loaf of bread dipped in sesame seeds. It would be accompanied by boiled eggs and zaatar.

We were dropped off right near the Damascus Gate. It really is a gate. If they wanted to, they could shut the doors. But to get to them, you had to walk down tens of stairs. If you will allow a funny story about the stairs first before I enter the gate. I was coming out of the Damascus Gate one time, trying not to look at the beggars lying on the side of the bridge that crosses a long dry moat before you get to the stairs when I saw a woman sitting on the stairs. That wasn't the remarkable thing, as there were hundreds of people sitting all over the half-moon-shaped stairs. The funny thing was she was exactly eye level with the thousands of people coming out of the gate and she was sitting in a short skirt with her legs wide open. I casually walked up to her so as not to startle her and whispered, "You are at eye level with all those people and your legs are apart." I didn't think a human could move that fast as she snapped her legs shut. All I could imagine was I would want someone to tell me, not just walk past.

There is nothing like the first time for anything, and this was no exception. All I could imagine was seeing the crusaders defending the city as Salaheddin attacked the walled city. I could see archers shooting from the killing holes down on the Infidels. I was walking on the same stones as so many historical figures. It was almost overwhelming, the sights, the smells, the crush of people. It was so frenetic.

Once you get past the actual door and into something like a portico, you then are flung into an open square area. The light is almost too much as you pass from the darkness into the light. Shops are on both sides but are so small and so full that seem to spill out onto the walkway by the sheer amount of stuff. Now you go down sloping long steps. It takes about three steps to cross just one step to the edge to go down to the next step. Going down is much easier than coming back.

At the bottom of this long 'road,' we then kept heading to our right. If you turn right when you get to the 'leather' area (the smell is almost overwhelming—remember what I said about smells being the best triggers?), you will run into the Church of the Holy Sepulchre.

During the reign of the Second Khalifa, Omar Ibn Al Khattab, he visited Jerusalem. At about Asr time (afternoon), it was time to pray while Omar was visiting the Church of the Holy Sepulchre. If he had prayed in the church, it would have been turned into a mosque, but he chose to leave the church and pray in an open area very near the church. This explains why there is a mosque very near this church. This ancient church is where Christians believe Christ was crucified and buried, and the church was built on top of the 'empty tomb.' It has been separated and controlled by Greek Orthodox, Armenian Apostolic, Coptic Orthodox, Syriac Orthodox, Ethiopian Orthodox, and Roman Catholic denominations for hundreds of years. A little-known fact is that the outer door (that is well over 20ft tall by 10 ft wide), is shut at night, is locked, and opened by the same Muslim family that has done it for over seven hundred years. Of course, I didn't know that at the time, and we just walked in with the rest of the people.

Most people were bending down to touch the stone they believed was where Christ's body was laid after he had been crucified—the Stone of Anointing. We just walked right on past as I was looking at all the different lamps hanging from the ceiling. It was very dark, and as there were priests swinging incense all over, it actually had a musty smell. We wandered around and found a staircase that led down. It wasn't roped off, and so we walked down the staircase.

I can't express my wonder and amazement at what we found. The rock wall following the curving staircase down was covered with thousands of little crosses carved into it. We would later learn that every Crusader carved a little 'Kilroy was here.' They were in the shape of a 'Greek Cross.' We followed the staircase down, and at the bottom, were rewarded with a beautiful mosaic floor.

I would learn later that it was dedicated to Saint Helena, but all I could do was walk around and stare down at me on the floor. Suddenly there was a little monk frantically showing me with his arms and whispering in a foreign language. I had no idea what he was trying to say, then he began pointing to the floor. I looked down, and I was standing on a beautiful ancient mosaic with my dirty shoes. I jumped so high that I scared myself. We would later visit again, and by now they had a rope at the top of the stairs so 'visitors' wouldn't even attempt going down where they weren't wanted. To this day, I have no idea where he came from; he just suddenly was there. After making our way back up the stairs and marveling at all the little crosses again, we followed the crowds to one of the holiest sites in Christianity—the Rock of Calvary (where Christians believe Christ was crucified). It was very crowded, and we wanted to see the rest of the city.

The old part of the city wound up and down long narrow corridors covered by a various amalgamation of materials: wood, corrugated tin, cloth, plastic tarp, just about anything to keep the water and sun out. We kept going west. We wandered past spice shops that were the most colorful and fragrant places. Meat shops with freshly butchered beef hanging from the ceiling on a hook. Souvenir shops selling all kinds of knick-knacks made of olive wood and mother-of-pearl. All those foreign tourists taking a piece of the 'holy land' back home.

We were wandering and not paying attention to where we actually were. We came out onto a gated area and almost stepped through the gate but were stopped by of all people a street cleaner. He spoke to my husband in Arabic. The gist of the conversation was on the other side of that doorway was the Wailing Wall, and if we were found to be Arab, it wouldn't go well for us. He told us to get away from here as fast as possible. Needless to say, we left even though I really wanted to peek at it.

We meandered back in the direction we had come. It's a funny thing, but to this day, I can tell what direction we were headed, and my husband knew a road or street or alley way from having been there once. We made a great team that way.

It was getting on in the day, and it was time to pray the noon prayer. We headed for 'Harim Al Sharif' the second most holy site in all of Islam. We were stopped at the checkpoint at the very small door that let you go out onto the complex. Because of our American passports, we were waved through. We were among the lucky ones. We would be able to do this many times, but others wouldn't be so lucky. The Dome of the Rock was absolutely breathtaking. The blue and white tiles, with the golden dome, were striking from even far away, but even more spectacular up close. I was lucky enough to pray in the Dome of the Rock, while my husband prayed in Al Aqsa Mosque. After the prayer, my husband rejoined me in the Dome of the Rock. I would learn about the name shortly. We waited for our turn and then we descended into the grotto.

It wasn't very big or wide, just a small cave under a huge rock in the middle of the mosque. We waited politely for the people to finish praying, and then we took our turn. I would later learn that the hole in the rock was where the prophet Mohammed (pbuh) ascended to heaven on his night journey when he traveled from Mecca to Jerusalem. The mosque was built much later to surround the rock. I didn't want to leave. It was so peaceful and quiet in there. But others were waiting for their turn so we went back up and spent some time just soaking in the surroundings. The inside dome was so awe-inspiring and peaceful. It was nothing like the medieval or Gothic churches I had visited. It might not be very bright inside, but it didn't have the oppressive feel like most cathedrals I'd visited.

We reluctantly left the Dome of the Rock because my husband wanted to show me the Al Aqsa Mosque. It was extremely plain on the interior. There was a large piece of wood propped up against a wall on the inside of the mosque. I was told this was the door that an Israeli had burned in 1969. I believe they kept it as a reminder about what had happened. I would visit the city many times, but there was only one first time.

Wadi Gaza

Picture a river wants to be. That was Wadi Gaza. It wasn't a river and didn't even qualify as a stream. What made it worse was that it was full of raw sewage as its only source of liquid. It was dumped into the ocean without being treated. Driving there was quite a journey. It was considered, at the time, the edge of the world from Gaza City. You couldn't drive straight to Khan Younis or Raffa from Gaza City as they were cut off by illegal Israeli settlements. This situation would only get worse with time, not better. So, Wadi Gaza was as far as it was 'safe' to travel. Did I mention that you had to drive through the water? This further complicated the situation, as you could only drive through when it was the dry season, or at least when the 'water' was low. There was a bridge over it, but it got blown up periodically and/or made useless. Now it is a major thoroughfare and you can drive straight to the border without a checkpoint. What a difference that makes!

Orphanage Retirement Home

I had never even given a thought to what happened to unwanted children. Where did they go? Who took care of them? In Islam, adoption is not allowed as you have no blood ties to the child so they can't inherit your money or property as such. Taking care of orphans is encouraged though. They are not of your blood, so how can they be around the opposite sex if they aren't related by blood? When posed with this idea, I had no answer for what happens to children who for any number of reasons aren't wanted by their families or have been orphaned by various tragedies. I would soon find out what happens to those in Gaza.

Through the tireless efforts of my father-in-law and many others who contributed not only money but also time, they were able to construct the place I was going to. My father-in-law was a founding member of the organization that made this possible. I was taken to the eastern edge of the strip. Not a far trip considering it was only seven miles wide. I went into a two-story building, and we climbed the stairs to the second floor. All my classes in high school, of which I had taken vocation education and had even been to the handicapped children's home, didn't prepare me for what I saw that day. I saw normal babies, I saw handicapped babies, but I mostly saw love. They were the product of a relationship that may or may not have been allowed, but they were being cared for.

This was on the first floor, but the ground floor was just as remarkable. It was filled with elder patients who didn't have any family to take care of them—it was a retirement home below an orphanage. In the middle of a culture that wholeheartedly believed in family and the sanctity of this body, there were people willing to look beyond the normal boundaries and help those who couldn't help themselves. I cried. I cried because I had been raised in a loving and caring family by parents who loved me and took care of me. I cried. I cried because my grandparents were getting older, but would be taken care of by their family until they literally couldn't physically do it anymore. I cried because there were people willing to go out of their way to make a life for others. I cried because I was pregnant with my first child, and he was totally wanted and loved.

End of June 1984

Remember when I said my husband had traveled on an 'entry permit'? We still had to seek permission for him to leave the Gaza Strip. We went every day for the last month of our stay. This was 1984. It wasn't the novel by Orwell, but it was damn close. Big Brother was everywhere. Big Brother controlled every movement you made. We loaded up a 1972 Volkswagen Bus and tried to take half the neighborhood to the beach one time, but ended up being pulled over by, what I came to understand later was, a 'collaborator.' This person was well-known by everyone and would later be one of the first people to be killed in the first Intifada. He pulled us over because there were too many people on the bus. Really? There were no seatbelt laws.

There weren't any traffic cops. There weren't any traffic lights. There were only collaborators who made your life hell. I had no idea what hell was like. I came from a small town, in a small state, in the Western United States. I was as white (and ignorant) as vanilla pudding.

But back to the permission saga. It became a daily ritual. We would walk to the compound where the Israeli army was set up and would ask to speak to the passport officer. After we had turned in my husband's re-entry permit, we were told to come back and pick it up. We had started early because the rumor was that it could take a long time to get the coveted permission to leave. Remember, these were people whose ancestry traced back thousands of years but were told they needed permission from an occupying army to enter or leave their own country.

Only 100 years earlier, there were no such things as borders, checkpoints, or even countries. People traveled back and forth as they pleased. In the early twentieth century, it was a common practice for a man from Gaza to go to Cyprus and get a bride who he brought home to Gaza. The family names of people from Gaza speak to the history of the strip: Turk, Hindi…But I digress. We got so known at the gate, that we would only approach, and the guard would turn us away with a flick of his hand. I was beginning to get alarmed. We had a plane reservation and no money to change it. Then I began to panic. It was two days from our ticket date. My husband refused to leave this time when the guard flicked at us. He insisted on speaking with the passport officer. We were finally admitted, but I had to wait outside in the sun.

He went into the trailer—her office. She had a stack of passports a mile high on her desk. My husband once again explained that we had a plane ticket out of Tel Aviv and that we needed permission to leave. The officer then said, "What is your wife's name?"

My husband said, "You don't have her passport because she's American." He would later tell me her face took on a completely different visage. Once she had heard I was 'American,' she stopped what she was doing, flipped through the tower of passports, found his, and promptly stamped it. Yes, just that fast and easy. Are you kidding? We had been coming every day in the hot sun, on foot, and it took all of two seconds.

To say we were a bit shocked is an understatement. To say that they deliberately made people suffer is a bigger understatement. But we had the long sought-after permission. Little did we know that this was only the beginning.

Unbeknownst to us was the fact that the Israeli army had in fact closed down the Erez checkpoint to all cars. Remember this was when anyone could drive their own personal car to Tel Aviv. This was pre-Intifada, pre-war, pre-everything worse to come. Being an American had proven to be an asset. Later, it would be a hindrance, but for now, it was a great asset and carried a lot of weight. So, we were on our way to the airport in the family van. We pulled up to the only way to describe it was a bottleneck. I should say that in point of fact, they were letting one car at a time through, but only one car, and that at a rate of about one every five minutes. We were in a sea of cars, hundreds in number. We were in a line in the middle of about ten lanes.

This would prove significant in a little while. I was freaking out because we were going to miss our plane if we stayed in this mess. I am not a world traveler as I have explained, and I had worn a short dress for the trip home. I had no scarf on my head and wouldn't wear the hijab for another ten years or so. I have blonde hair. So, in other words, stood out like a sore thumb.

This was a good thing sticking out. As I said earlier, I was freaking out. I couldn't just sit in a traffic jam and let the plane leave without me. I wanted to get home and get home now! Someone suggested that we go see if we could see the holdup. That's how far back we were. We couldn't even see the checkpoint at this stage because we were so far back in the jam. We both got out and began walking past the cars. Needless to say, a blonde girl wandering around this mess made more than one driver stick his head out of his car. When we finally reached the checkpoint, it was total chaos. Cars were trying to line up and jockey for a position, but as I said, they were letting only one car through at a time, and if they got angry, they would hold up the line. If they were feeling generous, they would let a few cars through at a time, then stop everyone and start letting another new line go. Remember I had said there were about 10 lines where we were, and there were about four here at the choke point. I was trying to stay calm but was panicking inside. At least I had remembered my passport. Never leave home without it became my mantra. Ever!

Of course, the soldiers were intrigued by a blondie in the short dress. And of course, they spoke English—they were Americans for the most part. They had been born in New York or somewhere in the United States and thought nothing of coming into a country they knew nothing about, had no roots too, kicked out the people who had been living there for millennia, and took up arms against them when they fought back. This is whom I was talking to. I was trying to explain my situation when a captain came over and yet again, I explained my situation—that I had a plane reservation from Tel Aviv and needed to catch it. He was more receptive than the first guy and asked which line my car was in. The VW van was somewhere in one of the two middle lines, but I hadn't paid attention to which line it was in, so they started to let both go, one line at a time. A few from this, and then a few from that. You can't imagine the faces of the drivers as they drove past a blondie directing traffic as I would yell, "Not that line, maybe this one?" Eventually, I saw the van and was able to get the whole line moving until they were at the gate. I jumped in and we were off again. We figured we had just enough time to still make the plane. Not!

About ten miles beyond the border, the van gave up the ghost. It died. Not out of fuel, not an overheated engine. It just died. It had given its all in the service of the family and decided right then and there to die. Are you kidding? I was about to blow a gasket when a car pulled up behind us. They were neighbors and had recognized the van. They offered to take us to the airport free of charge. I couldn't believe our luck. But this meant that heartfelt goodbyes were given on the side of the road as we hurriedly unloaded and loaded our luggage onto the waiting car. Not exactly the way we wanted to say goodbye but was just par for the course.

I don't remember anything about the trip to the airport except that as we pulled in, we saw a TWA plane taking off just over our heads. We knew instantly that we had missed our flight. There weren't that many planes taking off. So, we casually walked in to face the music as it were. They weren't happy about having to arrange another flight, but it really wasn't our fault that there was a pop-up check point placed on a busy road that morning. Remember when I said they didn't have that many flights? Just one a day. We would have to wait until the next day to take our flight to JFK. This left two choices. #1. Drive back to Gaza, hoping that the checkpoint wasn't in place again the next day, or even that they would let us in! #2. Stay in Tel Aviv.

We opted for the second, but that presented a whole new set of challenges. Where were we going to sleep? In a hotel—paying a huge amount of money for a taxi, then a hotel room, and then a taxi back to the airport. Oh, hell no! Remember the night in the border mosque? Well, you can add a night on the grass in front of the big letter airport sign. Yes, you read right on the grass. Why the grass? They wouldn't let us stay at the airport. Remember what I said about not too many flights? They weren't open 24-7 like now. They actually closed for the night. We were forced to sleep on the grass. But at least it was June—warm enough and not too many bugs.

And that wasn't the worst part about it. Once we were awake and back in line for our plane ride home, we were singled out yet again for 'extra screening.' Sound familiar? We were back in the special line where they unload your carefully packed suitcase before God and everyone, then x-ray your suitcase then bring it back, and then let you try to get everything back into it yet again. By the time we got through all this harassment, it was time to board the plane.

The flight home was a blur but was the reverse of the going. Stopping in Paris was eventful only in that we were 'held' in a special room until our next flight was ready to take off. I didn't get to see any of Charles De Gaulle's airports except that one room. It felt like we were being held hostage. And let's not forget that while you're waiting, you may need to use the restroom of which you have to pay for the privilege. Then off to New York.

JFK Airport

I'm sure I scared the border patrol guy. I had that look. I wanted to kiss him. He had said, "Welcome back to the United States." I had never heard such welcome words in my life. I was home. Or so I thought. Home is where the heart is, and my home was left in Gaza. It would pull and tug for the next 10 years, and eventually, we would move there. That's another story.

Part 2
To See While Dreaming

May 2002
Where in the world are we? Or where's Waldo?

We literally showed up on my mother's doorstep with six people and five suitcases. We were refugees with no place to go. We hadn't even stayed for the end of the school year exams because we were that desperate. I had no idea what we were going to do; only that we were safe. That's all I cared about. We had left our house, our friends, our family, our lives, but we were well out of harm's way. How did we get in harm's way? It was all my idea.

I loved teaching English as a Second Language. I got my first job after getting my bachelor's degree teaching ESL for a special Japan Airlines immersion course. I learned so much from that first job. I owe my entire career to that job. I even worked at the local college as an ESL instructor. After about a year and a half, I was informed that the college couldn't employ me any longer for their ESL classes as they were seeking accreditation, and all instructors needed to have a master's degree as a minimum. I didn't have one, so they let me go.

At about the same time, my husband was working for a famous insurance company and had even been made the assistant manager. There was only one problem. He had been bypassed not once, but twice to be the manager. We were both looking around for our next move. So why not move halfway around the world?

My in-laws had been talking about the apartment building they were building for a few years. It was almost complete, and they wanted to know which apartment we wanted. Of course, we hadn't taken it seriously until now. I couldn't teach without going back to school—I had no state teaching license, nor a master's degree. My husband was on a career path to nowhere. There was only one problem. The apartment building was in Gaza, Palestine.

Yes, you read right. Gaza. To put this in context, this was the spring of 1993. Our third child was a year old. I had no job. My husband was beginning to hate his, and the first Intifada was still going strong. I knew exactly what I was getting into because we had visited Gaza and the family in December 1991. Perhaps I should tell of that visit, and then you decide if you would pack up your family and move to such a place.

December 1991

It had been seven years since our first visit, although my husband had managed to make it to his sister's wedding, without me, in 1988. We had stayed for three months in 1984, but since my last visit, the first Intifada had begun. It would forever change the country and the family. My brothers-in-law would be arrested multiple times, general strikes would last for days at a time, and the threat of violence and death was around every corner. The most striking thing for me was that the Israelis had blocked roads and alleyways with fifty-five-gallon drums stacked on top of each other and held together with cement. They wanted to block off an escape route. So, it made it easier to 'catch' Palestinians. Obviously, the Palestinians tried to tear the walls down, but they would be put up again and the ones who had tried to pull them down would be informed on by those collaborators and put in jail.

Palestinians were not only occupied but also harassed and shot at will on any pretense. Strikes were a weekly occurrence. Arrests were rampant for any pretext or pretense. Actually, I believe we wanted to visit his family before any of them were killed.

We arrived at the Tel Aviv Airport to be manhandled and our suitcases searched before they finally let us through, and we were able to catch a taxi to Gaza. It was the same orange glow from the lights on our way to the family house. I loved the smell of orange groves. It wasn't as prominent, but it was still there. You had to drive way out to an isolated farm just to get that smell, now that there were so few.

We had to stop at the 'international' border of Erez. We were asked about the nature of our visit, which this time was just a visit. I don't remember being held up too long, but I'm sure they were questioning our reasons.

When we finally arrived, we were greeted by the immediate family and by my American sister-in-law. She had married my husband's younger brother. The brothers were only eighteen months apart. It was nice seeing a person I could actually talk to. Actually, I think she was relieved to see me as she had someone to talk to. It had been a difficult four years for her. She had lived through the entire Intifada, each and every step of the way. Our family house was half a block away from Shifa Hospital, the site of the opening volley in the first Intifada.

Intifada

This is how it started…On 9 December 1987 near Jabaliya Refugee Camp, an IDF (Israeli Defense Force) truck collided with a civilian car killing all four Palestinian passengers. This sparked protests, and reprisals from both sides, with all the causalities being brought to the only 'trauma' hospital in the whole of the Gaza Strip. This would become significant in that the people waiting to see who lived and who didn't make it would grow in number and size. Our family home was half a block away. When the number reached a critical mass, the IDF decided that they had seen enough and used tear gas to disperse the crowd. Aerosol doesn't know the difference between the hospital grounds and the houses next to it. The wind blew it straight for our house where my American sister-in-law was pregnant. They kept the windows shut and tried not to breathe in the gas. This was the war that 'invented' the 'dumb dumb' bullet that was marketed as non-lethal. Picture a projectile made of a hard steel ball bearing encased by 'rubber.' Non-lethal? Yes, if you don't shoot someone in the head, or leg artery, or vital organ, etc. Oh, and just because someone loses a leg or an eye in the process, remember it's non-lethal!

As fate would have it, we would call the next day, 10 December to announce the birth of our second child (a boy), and they said they announced the birth of the Intifada. It would continue until my arrival many years later, but just keep in mind that this whole time, Palestinians were being harassed and killed on a daily basis. My husband would visit in 1988, but it was too last to keep his residency card. He traveled as an American and that would seal our fate.

Back to the visit, even though I was six months pregnant, I was doing well. It was just getting harder to move around, but we managed. They even gave us a bedroom to sleep in, so we were the four of us in one room in a house full of people sleeping all over the place—in the living room, on the veranda, all over. It was so much fun to be surrounded by so many people.

There were two events that would forever change us during this month-long visit. The first was when my husband went to a 'cultural' show being held in the only stadium in the city at the time. Normally, this was used for football matches, but on this day, it was being used for this show. It wasn't overly political, but after the show where the Palestinian flag was being flown in complete defiance of the Israeli military, it would turn violent. The Israeli army wasn't about to let the audience march off in a demonstration of Palestinian defiance. How could they let the people they were brutally occupying be allowed to display national unity for a country that didn't exist? So naturally, when a moving object runs into a non-movable object, something has to give.

My husband found himself in the middle of this protest gone wrong with these 'bullets' firing all around him. It was total chaos. He managed to get behind a light pole and stand straight up hoping that a stray bullet didn't find him. Most of him was probably visible, but he was lucky. He was standing there when a man running by him was hit by a live bullet (not even a dumb dumb one) and fell near him. By now the shooting had started to become sporadic and not as intense, so my husband ran over to the man. He had been shot in the back with a bullet coming out the front. My husband applied pressure to the wound and tried to hold the man's intestines while screaming for help. An ambulance was nearby, and he helped them load him into it. You can imagine my shock and horror at seeing my husband covered in blood when he managed to get home safely after dropping off the injured man at Shifa Hospital. I couldn't believe that people actually lived like this every day.

The second event happened at around the time of curfew. Any time there was a confrontation, shooting, or any general demonstration, the army would impose a curfew. This would happen quite often and was only to disrupt and harass the locals. This meant that everyone had to be off the streets by eight o'clock. If you were caught out after the curfew, the army wouldn't hesitate to shoot you on sight. I would find this out personally.

It was close to the time of curfew, and I assumed my oldest son was with his uncles in the sweet shop a couple of houses around the corner from where we were staying. Most of the houses on our block had shops on the first floor, and apartments above them. This helped defray the cost of the building. The family business of sweets was started by my husband's grandfather back in 1912 after learning about them from a Lebanese man before starting his own shop with his brother. Upon the death of my husband's grandfather, my husband's father had to leave university and take over the family business with his cousin as there was no one else who could. During the Intifada, it was impossible to travel from the family house to the original sweet shop located downtown as there were too many strikes and curfews. So, they had relocated to a shop around the corner from the family house. It wasn't as popular, but it was at least open. My father-in-law worked in the shop all his life, but when the sons got old enough, they started to do most of the day-to-day work.

It was dark and only about half an hour to the curfew. Most people start to finish whatever they are doing in order to be home before the set time. I had assumed my oldest son was helping his uncles clean up the shop when we got a fateful phone call. The relatives that owned the building where the sweet shop was, called to tell us that several jeeps and troop transport trucks had pulled up in front of the shop. They knew this because they lived right above the shop with their windows overlooking the street and the sound of several troop trucks and jeeps was hard to miss.

The next minute was utter chaos. My mother-in-law was screaming and shouting and running around trying to find something to wear on her head to go down. I finally got the gist from my English-speaking sister-in-law and grabbed my American passport on the way downstairs. I couldn't put into words how much adrenaline must have been coursing through my veins. Remember, I was six months pregnant, but boy, I moved quickly that night.

By the time we got to the corner, I could hear many voices shouting and yelling. I didn't hesitate and kept running the one hundred yards to the front of the shop. Israeli soldiers were swarming around, and I couldn't locate my mother-in-law at first. I found her, and she was quite shaken up, mostly from the mad dash down the stairs and around the corner. The soldiers were in a frenzy because they couldn't find anyone. My brothers-in-law had heard the jeeps coming and skipped over the back wall behind the shop. Actually, it was only one brother. The brother that I thought had my son. Somehow, I learned that no one had seen my son. My brother-in-law wouldn't have taken my son as he was only six years old and would slow him down. But my son was nowhere to be seen.

I was running around like a chicken with my head cut off and soon found myself in front of a troop carrier. The engine was still on, but I was like a deer in the headlights, literally! I wouldn't move until someone talked to me, but to my shock and horror, the driver actually gunned the engine and lurched forward in order to scare me. I swear I had a flash of the cartoons I had watched since I was a small child. Me lying flat on the ground with a tire tread running the length of my body with the tire tread going right over the top of my American passport. Eventually, I quit playing chicken with the troop truck as someone suggested that my son may be in the back of the troop carrier as they routinely pick up young boys to scare them. So now my goal was getting the back of the truck that had just threatened me.

I started running around asking if anyone had seen my son. I was yelling he's six years old. The only response I got from any of the soldiers was, "Oh, you want sex?" Yes, you read that correctly. I actually had an Israeli soldier as if, I, six months clearly pregnant, wanted to have sex. I was shocked, but now I was mad. I was determined more than ever to see the back of that damn truck. Eventually, I made my way to the back. It was empty! Empty! They had neither my son nor my brother-in-law. Score one for the good guys. After about an hour, they decided to give up and drive off in a huff. Good riddance to bad rubbish.

I was now frantic to find my son. If he wasn't being held by the soldiers, where in the world was he? Actually, he had gotten bored from the sweet shop and was in the ground floor apartment, below where we were staying, visiting his great uncle. My brother-in-law was in the house, safe and sound.

So, between my husband getting shot at, and me almost getting run over by the troop carrier, it was a most eventful visit. I would go home and deliver the most beautiful baby girl. We would live for another year and a half before I made that fateful decision.

We were stuck, me with no job; him with a nowhere job. Yes, we had the 2.1 children, the house, three cars, the backyard with the swing and the barbecue, the soccer games, and even piano lessons. We had the American dream. Not. I couldn't teach without a license, and he would never get beyond assistant manager unless he went to another company and started at the bottom all over again.

I knew how to teach English as a Second Language (ESL). Yes, I had only done it for a year and a half, but I had one of the best teachers ever. She taught me how to explain the nonsense of English grammar and spelling. As a native speaker, we know instinctively how sentence structure works, but to be able to explain why to a non-native speaker is a whole different animal. I will be forever grateful to her.

She gave me my career. As an ESL teacher, I could work anywhere in the world, including the Middle East, and especially Gaza. They didn't have access to any outsiders, no one to practice on, and they certainly didn't have access to books! That would prove the most difficult part about teaching there, the lack of resources, but I wouldn't discover that until much later.

So, I could be an ESL teacher, but what would my husband do? He probably wouldn't be able to work in insurance, so what would he do? He didn't want to work in the family business, he had avoided it all these years, so what was the alternative? He had been active in sports his whole life and had a special affinity for tennis as of late. He had an American passport, so he would be able to travel to Israel and bring back equipment of all kinds.

We had a plan. There was only one problem. We had the house, three cars, and his job. He would need time to divest of all of these. And would I be able to live there? Did I want to live there? Could I get along with the large family and all that that entails? We would soon find out.

August 1993 What Was I Thinking?

I took two whole boxes of books and toys. The boys were young, and my daughter was only eighteen months old. I needed comfort, and so did they. My husband would stay and sell everything else and join us in six months. It would be the longest six months of my life.

I didn't speak Arabic; my in-laws didn't speak English. But I did have my American sister-in-law. She would act as our translator for a while. The first order of business was registering the children for school. My oldest son would be going into third grade. My second son would be entering first grade. My daughter would eventually go to a pre-school. My second son was easy to get into the local public school as everyone was entering school at that age and didn't know how to read or write Arabic. That school didn't have any openings for third grade. We knew this after visiting the Ministry of Education. The ministry was in a building that resembled more of a jail than a ministry. Stairs covered by asbestos (Zingo in the local vernacular). I have no idea what was said, but the gist was no room at the inn. This would create a unique problem for us. Where to put my oldest son? There were really only two private schools available. One was run by the Orthodox Christians, so of course, we chose the other one. My mother-in-law went with me to try and get my son into this exclusive and private school. We met the owner and had a nice little chat, none of which I understood until the owner addressed me in English.

The first stumbling block was that he was entering third grade but couldn't read or write a word of Arabic. How did we imagine he would progress when all the subjects; math, science, history, geography, social studies, everything except English was given in Arabic? My mother-in-law said we would get a private tutor and by three months into the year, they could test him and if he wasn't on par, we would take him out. That was a great idea, but there was more. The owner wasn't stupid. He asked me what I do for a living, and I replied that I was an ESL teacher. He said he would agree to take my son, but only if I would teach English at the school. He had us over a barrel. I had to agree, but thankfully, I had already secured a full-time position at the

Islamic University of Gaza, thanks in large part to my father-in-law, so I could only teach one or two classes a day. That would work out as I could go to the university in the morning, run to the school in the afternoon, and bring my son home with me.

The seventh-grade boys' class was the worst—aren't all middle school-age boys? They were rowdy, noisy, full of boy energy and no place to get rid of it; stuck in a stuffy classroom all day when all they really wanted was to be out in the fresh air playing football or just goofing off. They pushed all my buttons, and one day I couldn't take it anymore. So, I called for the principal, and he came and literally beat you-know-what out of a boy. I was so mad at the boy and myself for having pushed me to such measures. I would never do that again, no matter how bad the class got. It was better after that though…they had learned my limits, and I, theirs. I would walk into a dress shop 25 years later to have a grown man call me by name. I couldn't place him if my life depended on it, but he said I had been his teacher in seventh grade. And he remembered me with a fondness I probably didn't deserve, but we tend to remember only the good stuff and throw the rest away.

I will never forget my oldest son's first day of school. We had arranged for a bus to stop in front of the house and pick him up. We hadn't paid any attention to the goings on around us and were wondering why the bus was taking so long to come. Little did we know that in actuality, there had been a general strike called, and in point of fact, there were no children on the bus. That should have been our first clue. I put him on the bus and watched as it drove down to the end of the street. I heard gunfire and ran back to open the door to the street just in time to see the bus make a huge U-turn and come back the wrong way up our street. He was followed by a small tank-looking vehicle. The bus stopped and I grabbed my son off of it and we ran into the alley leading to our house door. We ran up the stairs and out on the veranda just in time to see boys running toward that same tank, throwing rocks. Believe me, when I say, I paid attention to what was happening and never sent him on the bus if there was to be a strike.

I got another job. It was at the local university; it was one of the best jobs I've ever had. I was a native English speaker, teaching young women all about the English Language. I had a group that was in their last semester of university and about to graduate in English. So, what the heck, let's study poetry! It's about as English as it gets, right? Only if you're going to study the Romantic Poets, you need a lot of background as they refer to many different areas: Greek mythology, the Bible, history, politics, and just about every subject under the sun. Wait, Greek mythology? The Bible? My students had not the slightest idea about these subjects. How could I teach Byron or Shelly without first teaching these? Ok, I couldn't teach the Bible, but I could say this was what it was referencing. It was one of the most memorable and hardest semesters I would ever teach.

I would go on to teach architects, engineers, and, of course, ESL classes, but this will remain one of the best classes, ever. I must digress just a bit. Remember I was by myself, alone with the kids, and waiting for my husband to come after selling all our belongings. I was going up the stairs to the bedroom in the old house where I and the kids slept when I tripped. I didn't think much of it at the time, but after a couple of days, and it still hurt, I was thinking about getting it x-rayed.

This would involve the logistics of dragging my English-speaking sister-in-law, getting a car to take us to the clinic, finding a doctor, x-rays, etc. I complained about my pain during my class with those last semester students, and one student piped up that I should come to see her grandmother. Ok, I was thinking about how a grandmother could help my aching arm, but I was curious and wanted to see how she lived. I love grandmothers and mine had saved my life. They have all the love and wisdom that comes with a full life. I would have to travel to the northern area Beit Lahyia and eventually, I found her house even without GPS. I was greeted and welcomed by the whole family. The most interesting part was when I was given 'fire-brewed' coffee. This is the coffee that is heated on an open flame usually in the front yard, or in the center courtyard of the family home. I was told that they hadn't emptied this particular pot in over 100 years. So, theoretically, I was drinking 100-year-old coffee. They only add to it, boil it, and serve. I was a bit freaked out, but it would get weirder.

I was introduced to the grandmother. She asked me where I hurt, and I told her my left arm. She asked for some olive oil, and she rubbed my arm. Not too hard, but hard enough. Then she wrapped it with a very dirty-looking cloth and told my student to tell me that not only was it not broken, but it would be fine in a couple of days. I left the wrap on overnight, and would you believe she was right? It was much better the next day after really hurting and scaring me. Trust your grandmothers, they know everything!

Those were some of the best times. I was totally alone, but I learned that I could do anything. Get a job, put the kids in school, and get another job. My husband came for a visit to check it out. Could we really do this? Would we really do this? Yes, let's do this. He would go back to the United States and sell the house, the cars, the furniture, and quit his job and cash in his 401-K. We were headed out of town, and we weren't coming back! At least for a while...

October 1993 "Open the Door or We'll Knock It Down"

Welcome to the Intifada!

I was sleeping in a corner bedroom of the old family villa with my three kids, and my sister-in-law and her husband and kids were in another room with the rest of the family which at that time included five brothers-in-law and our parents-in-law. It was a rather full house, to say the least. Consequently, to be rudely awakened in the middle of the night by the pounding on the front door by Israeli soldiers gets your blood flowing and fast let me tell you. I had no idea what they were doing; let alone what they were looking for. Turned out that they were looking for any money or gold they could find. They said it was weapons, but trust me, back then, no one even had the resemblance of a gun or weapon. They could take it, and you had to go to an Israeli court to petition to get it back. Yeah right.

They emptied my sister-in-law's closet and went through all the pockets on all the coats and jackets. They were so thorough. I would never have thought to hide stuff where they were looking. Later I found out that the family treasure (gold) was actually hidden under the latest baby under the baby mattress. Take that, you sneak thieves in the night. We would get many of those harassing visits, but more about that later. On to better and happier times.

January 1994

If I'm going to live in a new house, I need to furnish it! What better way than with some used furniture? A road trip will fit the bill. We can go to the old city of Yafa and to the used market there—fill up a truck and away we go. Obviously, it's never that easy, but I did fill up most of a truck by buying beds for three kids, a fridge, and a desk. And of course, my mother-in-law couldn't resist the prices so she bought a lot of stuff. We were paying for a truck, so let's fill it up!

About this time, my brother-in-law would actually save the life of an Israeli doctor caught in the wrong place at the wrong time. Demonstrations and skirmishes were the order of the day. My brother-in-law was driving into one of these and saw the mob about to tear apart a man caught in one of these. He turned out to be a doctor, but my brother-in-law didn't know or care. He saw a man about to be killed and did the right thing. This same brother-in-law would go on to be targeted by the Israeli military and would be assassinated by them for his activities in the second Intifada, but I got ahead of myself. He needs to get married first.

February 1994 Moving and Marriage

The big day had arrived. Ok, actually two big days had arrived. After my husband had visited in November of 1993 and gone back to sell everything we owned—the house, the cars, the furniture, he came for the wedding. We got to move into our almost finished apartment. It had no windows, and it was a cold and wet February in Gaza, but it was ours! And we got to be alone at last. Ok, not alone, we were in a building full of people, and it would soon grow very quickly with births and marriages. Speaking of marriages, that brother-in-law who saved the Israeli doctor was getting married. Why was this a big deal? Because this would be my mother-in-law's first real wedding—not! There was a minor slip-up when he was engaged to another girl, but we don't mention that fact. Second, the actual wedding party where the women get to dance and laugh and twirl in their new dresses—not! This would be a very solemn and formal occasion as the bride's family would have nothing to do with music and dancing. They were even stricter religiously than my mother-in-law who was one of the first to actually start wearing a scarf back in the 1970s. Most women didn't even know to wear one, and she was one of the first to start dressing modestly. Therefore, it came as quite a shock that we weren't strict enough! Really?

We did get to dance, but that was only the very close family women in a small apartment in our building. Not the royal entrance and ball my mother-in-law had dreamed of forever. I married the oldest, so, there was that belated party on the roof after one year of marriage. The next son married an American too. Small party after the fact as well. The third child was my husband's sister and she got married shortly after the first Intifada started, so again no big celebration. So here comes number four. And it's a bust again. She would have to wait for number five, and number seven to get her big parties. Number six married an Egyptian girl and there was a party, but because she wasn't from Gaza, only a quarter of the city showed up. Number eight would marry a lady from Peru and that party was even smaller than mine. There were only my parents-in-law, the bride and groom, my mother, and my husband. A couple of the bride's friends eventually showed up to wish the happy couple good luck.

Back to the newlyweds. They would only be married for two months before my brother-in-law would be hauled away and tortured for eight months. Can you imagine being a new bride and for eight months you look forward to the monthly shakedown and humiliation before you get to see your new husband across from you separated by 100 yards and a couple of chain link fences? You have to shout to be heard. Holding hands was not allowed and you couldn't reach him even if you tried. This was your new reality. He would be released and then imprisoned and tortured numerous times. As a result, is it any wonder that he devoted himself to making and producing weapons? Eventually, this would cost him his life.

Someone ratted him out and sprayed the car he traveled in to be targeted by a missile. It didn't matter that there were three other people with him in the car. It didn't matter that there was an innocent pedestrian minding his own business walking down the street when they blew up the car. They identified my brother-in-law by the hand they found up in a tree about 50 feet from the bombed car. He had an accident while making sweets when much younger and had actually ground off the tip of a finger. That's how they knew it was him, from the missing tip on the finger. But again, I'm going too fast.

March 1994 "The Return"

I had only been here in Gaza for seven months, but I could tell what was about to happen was a big deal. For Palestinians, this would be the one and only big day. It would all go downhill literally, but for the moment, they got to cheer. When I decided to come to Gaza in the summer of 1993, we had no idea what was about to happen. The Oslo Peace Accord would be announced in September after I'd already come here. Yasser Arafat, the leader of the Palestinian Liberation Organization, would be coming home!

I had never given much thought to the symbolism that is held by raising a flag. Since I was a schoolgirl, we'd said the pledge of allegiance daily, I stood for the national anthem and crossed my heart with all the patriotism I could muster as a girl who had never given any thought to who had paid for that flag or national anthem. During the occupation, the Palestinian flag would be flown surreptitiously and without ceremony removed and trashed by Israeli soldiers. So, for the entire Gaza Strip, one million people, it was about three flags to every person! Arafat was going to land in Raffa, the town on the southern border with Egypt, by helicopter, then go by motorcade through all the little towns and villages to finally arrive in the mother city—Gaza.

We watched the landing on T.V. And heard all the shouts and noise as the motorcade got closer. Our house wasn't that far from his eventual compound and the shouts continued well into the night. This honeymoon would be as short-lived as my brother-in-law's. Yes, there was prosperity for a few. Yes, there was some freedom of movement, but again for a limited few. He had only succeeded in getting most of Israelis out of most of the Gaza Strip. There would be a settlement in the middle of the strip for the next 18 years! This would stifle traffic, and if there was any ruckus the only road connecting the north with the south of the strip could be arbitrarily closed and you could find yourself on the wrong side of that imposed border! More than once, I wouldn't have a class because my students couldn't come to the city as the road had been shut. Why? God only knows. It was part of the larger torture Gazans had learned to endure.

June 1994 See the Other Half

One of the many trips we would 'have to' make just to renew our 'visitor' visa. My husband had not been able to return in 1987 when all residency permits were canceled and if you wanted a new one, you had to come within a six-month period and apply for one. We couldn't afford to send him at that time, and his I.D. lapsed. He was born here, lived here for 18 years, and for that six-month period couldn't come home so he would never be able to return? Really? And in Israel, it didn't matter where you were born as long as you came and professed your religion, you could be given citizenship and even hold dual citizenship. This included the government as well. Most countries did not allow someone to be a dual and hold a governmental position as this could lead to a conflict of interest. But Israel led the way with dual citizenship holders. I've always wondered if Israel was the promised land, why do they still keep their other citizenship?

Why? Because they know that the land they hold has been stolen and could be taken back at any moment! They have no moral or legal claim. Palestinians were here before they came, were here when they were here, and were here after they left! Up until about 100 years ago, there weren't even international borders. People traveled as they pleased, and stayed where they wanted, not worrying about passports, I.D. Cards, citizenship. There was a train from Gaza to Cairo until the late 1960s. Now it takes more than two days sometimes to make that same trip.

We took the family to Cyprus. The Turkish side of Cyprus. This was back when there was theoretically a border dispute and tensions were at an all-time high. Greeks and Turks have fought for millennia—Trojan War, ring a bell? Troy has been found to be a city in Turkey. Helena was a Greek lady from Sparta. We saw and walked up to the dividing line and could see over the barbed wire. It looked no different than the Turkish side. Why do people hate 'the other' when they are so close in background, culture, and beliefs? We pick on what makes us different, but we aren't that different. Cats and dogs are further apart than humans are to one another. We are one species, Humans. Get over it!

We narrowly avoided the topless beach, and the ice cream shop lady tried to eat my husband with her eyes, but all in all, we had a good time. Lugging around three children was not my idea of a good time, but we all needed to get our passports stamped, so family vacation anyone?

January 1995 Laid Off

I had been teaching for a year and a half when I was called into the dean's office. It was fairly routine, and I didn't think anything of it at the time. I had been doing well, and the students liked me. I was politely told that because of the 'peace,' a whole lot of people had returned in hopes of a new beginning, and that included some very educated 'men.' So, what did that have to do with me? I am a native speaker, an educated woman who knows how to teach English, but I was told there were men 'who need the job more than you.' Really? Just because you got your master's in Shakespeare doesn't make you a good teacher! But alas, I was politely and quietly let go. I had quit jobs before but had never been 'let go.' I loved that job. I certainly didn't want to teach middle or high school kids. I'd tried it and didn't like it. Their way of teaching was too corporal. And if you didn't teach that way, you'd get run over. The kids were too used to that method of teaching. So, now what?

I wasn't too worried as my husband had opened up his own sporting goods store. It wasn't much, but he would make it work. He could travel to Israel and buy sporting goods—soccer balls, shoes, fishing gear, tennis rackets and balls, weightlifting equipment, just about anything and bring it back. The hard part was negotiating a good price. He needed to make a profit, but his margin was very small. The store was located in the old sweet shop where his father used to make kunafa (an Arabic sweet)—the family business. He made tens of trips, but as the years rolled on, getting out of the Gaza Strip would become harder and harder.

Consequently, we had an income and didn't have a house or car payment, so we weren't going to starve, but I'd worked since I was 16 and couldn't imagine being a housewife. The only thing I knew how to do was teach English. So, I could teach, but where? As I said, I refused to teach in a school, so I did the very next best thing. We opened up our own private teaching institute: PALI—Palestinian American Language Institute in the space between the two apartment buildings where we lived. Talk about an easy commute! There was even a built-in storage area for the books we would eventually print down in the basement. I hate basements. Why? Because when I was growing up, we had a basement. That wasn't it. It was because this basement was forever flooding with water!

So much so that it had mushrooms growing in it! But I would put on my father's work boots (waterproof) and trudge down to get a jar of whatever was stored down there. I can still remember my father commenting that this one jar was the last of my grandmother's canning. My grandmother could can anything! I mean anything. Meat, fruit, vegetables, pickles—sour bread and butter. Her bread and butter pickles were to die for! We used the basement because it was fairly dry, dark, and cold. Great for storage and mushrooms.

Summer 1968

Speaking of canning, one time while visiting my paternal grandparents at their home, my brother and cousins were sitting on the back porch of their house. They were all toddlers, and no one thought much about them getting into mischief but, of course, that was faulty thinking. There were glass jars sitting there waiting to be used in another round of canning that hadn't started yet. Being little boys, they were rowdy and somehow managed to knock off one of the jars—it broke in half with the sharp edges sticking straight up. How do we know all this? Because my little brother managed to fall onto the jar face first! Yes, you read correctly, face first onto the broken jar. He missed his eye by a hair's breadth. He had two sharp cuts one above the eye in his eyebrow and the other to the side of his mouth. His scream brought everyone running because of course, it was a cry from the depths of his little heart.

I can remember my uncle coming running around the corner to show us the damage! There was blood everywhere as you are wont to get with a head cut! Would you believe Grandma and Grandpa lived next to a hospital? You can't make this stuff up. So there goes my uncle with blood all over his shirt, carrying my brother through the hedge to get stitched up. As a big girl of five, I thought he was dying! I'd never seen so much blood. Of course, an hour later he toddled back with two band-aids covering his face. Mom said the girls would think that was quite sexy when you're older. Looks like you were in a sword fight! Right! I was comforted by Grandma. She always seemed to be able to calm me down. Sadly, all her recipes died with her! Not one survived beyond her death from cancer. She had saved my life (more about that later-*Adam*) and on some level, I knew that in my bones. I loved her so much. I would take comfort and enjoy my other grandmother for many years after that.

Back to Pali. It was so easy. No license or inspection was required. Just word of mouth. Yes, I only had a few students at first, but because my students were actually learning from a native speaker, I gained lots of students and was able to open up several different levels. Around the second year, I became pregnant but that didn't stop me from teaching right up until I had the baby. I would have to take some time off, but that is all explained in *Adam*. The only hard part about the institute was the administrative headaches; printing, registering, payments, and contacting missing students. Eventually, we hired a secretary (my husband's cousin) to come man the front desk. It was a heady time. I was the master of my own destiny. I was the leader of my own ship. I was woman! Obviously, this wouldn't last, but I enjoyed it while it did.

June 1995 Beach Vacation Anyone?

Once again, we are off to the wilds of Cairo for a little rest and relaxation. Not. It was to renew our 'visit' visa yet again. This was becoming a royal pain. You had to pay to leave, pay to come back in and forget about all the travel expenses, hotel, taxis, food, and misc. It's the miscellaneous that would kill you every time. We had a nice little visit in Cairo and had even taken a few of the extended family with us, my mother-in-law and a couple of unmarried brothers-in-law. The misc. took the shape in that the border was suddenly closed to foreign people trying to cross the border back into Gaza. Only residents are allowed. What? Are you kidding? Not allowed back in. Why, for Pete's sake? Because unbeknownst to us, there had been an assassination attempt on Hosni Mubarak's life in Sudan. He had escaped, but the country was on high alert.

Hosni Mubarak had become president upon the assassination of Anwar Sadat, so they had reason to be very cautious and nervous. But to close the border just like that?

And it gets worse. My husband needed to return and somehow, he convinced them he was a resident. The kids and I weren't. Hence, my mother-in-law volunteered to stay with us. We were able to get a chalet near the beach, but the T.V. was in mourning mode and didn't show anything except pictures of the 'alive' president for a week! Yes, we went swimming but you can only take so much sand and the beach! Ask my poor mother-in-law after having a jellyfish attack her face. She was in so much pain for a week after that.

After two weeks, I was getting stir-crazy. I didn't speak much Arabic, and my mother-in-law no English. It was a quiet vacation. My husband finally called in a favor and got a relative in the Palestinian Authority (PA) to use his influence to get my special permission to come back in. We hardly ever used such help called 'wasta' in Arabic. But precisely because we didn't use it or abuse it, we were able to use it when we really needed it, see *Adam*.

March 1996 Family Vacation-Again

As we were wont to do, we had to leave for our six-month visa renewal. This would be a special trip as I would finally get to see only the second most sought-after item on my bucket list—Petra, Jordan. The first on the list, of course, were the pyramids of Giza and the Cairo Museum. But first, we needed to visit family and see the city of Amman. We were five people, so the cheapest way to get around town was on a microbus that stopped at specific places and went to specific areas of the city. You just waited until your bus happened along. We got up one morning and were going to another part of the city. Therefore, we waited for our bus. We all climbed on and then all hell broke loose. Our youngest, who is our only daughter, by the way, started screaming like a banshee. We had forgotten her blanket 'ninny.' Think Linus from the Peanuts comic strip. She wouldn't go anywhere without it. We had to stop the bus, yes really, stop the bus and get off and go back and get it. I know what you're thinking that she grew up to be a very spoiled brat. Actually, quite the opposite. She's a very accomplished wife and mother who thinks of all others before herself. But that was after the blanket 'ninny' mysteriously disappeared at home one day a little while after this trip. Years later, she would discover it and take it to her home. She still has it, by the way.

We ended up taking a private taxi to Petra and staying quite a bit away from the ancient site. They hadn't built hotels too close to it. I could hardly stand myself as we got closer. We were told by the locals that to get to the 'treasury,' it would be quite a hike, and would we like to ride a horse there? Uh no. I was seven months pregnant (yes, I love to travel while pregnant) and that would not be a good idea to go bouncing around on a horse. I grew up on horses but hadn't ridden in a long time and knew that especially pregnant women shouldn't ride unless they've been doing it all along. It just so happened that they had a rather rickety old buggy that I could ride in. Calling it a buggy is giving it more character than it's worth. It was a cart on wheels. No shock absorbers at all. I think the horse would have been better!

But I forgot all about that when I was careening down a very narrow passage with super high walls of sandstone—

think Zion National Park in Utah—on either side and suddenly right in front of you is a three-story structure carved completely in stone. Words do not do it justice! Abruptly, it's there! It took my breath away. Now I had to get out of the damn cart! Gracefully! Not! But once I got my breath back, all I could do was stare. What skill? What artistry? So much time and effort and for what? We are still guessing. The word 'treasury' was a misnomer. It was too small to be a house, yet so elegant and marvelous that it couldn't be ignored. We may never know what it was exactly. It was just beautiful.

To be honest, I had thought that Petra was just the treasury. But in reality, it was quite a large ancient site as I was to find out the hard way. We were told, again, by the locals that there were more things to see further in. We walked about 500 yards and came upon a sign pointing up a hill saying citadel. A citadel? What do you think? We finally asked someone how long a hike and they said maybe half an hour or so. Yes, let's. About two steps into the hike, our daughter wanted to be carried as she suddenly found herself too tired to walk. She was three. Not too heavy, but heavy enough. My poor husband had to carry her all the way up as I was in no condition to be carrying a three-year-old. I had enough to carry by myself. And I did.

We got passed on the way up by a man leading a donkey carrying water bottles and other things to sell. We were slightly encouraged by this as there must be something worth seeing if he was going our way too. You guessed it. There was a pile of rocks at the top that said behind a very sad-looking sign—citadel. Not even a good-looking or organized pile of rocks. Not in the shape of anything. Just a pile of rocks. Oh no. We'd climbed the damn hill for this? We bought a couple of bottles of water and thought about going back down the way we had come from. The man with the donkey suggested that we go down the other side. What other side? The other side of the hill took you down to the forum. What forum? "You'll see," he said. Thus, we went down the other side. Let's just say, this side was way worth the climb. Forget the pile of rocks. We saw all the little caves carved into the side of the mountain. They weren't sure what these were used for either as most were quite small, but they could have been sleeping quarters, or houses. The highlight for me was when we stopped at the 'Lion Fountain.'

When it rained, the rain poured down and came out of the mouth of a lion carved into the side of the hill. Literally a relief of a lion in stone, but the better part was the ancient Bedouin woman, and I do mean an ancient little lady selling trinkets next to the fountain. She had bits of jewelry, necklaces made of stones, key chains, bits, and bobs laid out on a blanket. Of course, I bought something. I don't remember what, but I made sure we gave her some money for sitting in the sun and hauling all that up the trail every day. We had a riotous time coming down the other side when again we saw a site to absolutely take your breath away.

A huge and I mean huge Roman amphitheater laid before us. It wasn't the Forum, but who cares? It was Roman and no doubt about it. Once you got down and walked around it, it wasn't the same as seeing it from a distance. But by now, I was completely exhausted. I couldn't walk another step, and neither could my daughter. We were both wiped out. Go. Leave us. Save yourselves. Another local Bedouin to the rescue. He was leading a camel and I gladly accepted. I had my daughter in front of me, and I tried to hang on for dear life. If you've never ridden a camel, I'll try to explain the locomotion.

First, it's sitting on the ground. You gently climb on, and this is usually behind the hump. Arabian camels only have one hump. Asian camels have two. So, you're behind the hump hoping you don't casually slide off the back. Therefore, to stand up the camel actually raises its hind legs first so you're thrown forward and about the time you think for sure you're going for its neck, it then rocks you back to begin to raise its front legs. Now for sure, you think you're going off the back to the ground in a most ungracious manner. But suddenly you are flat and still on the camel. Really? Not lying on the ground spread eagle? You know why they call the camel the ship of the desert? Because they rock just like a boat! Back and forth and back and forth. Between the baby that I was carrying and my little girl in front of me, I got squished so badly that I thought I would give birth right then and there. But the worst was yet to come. We had to stop and get off. Oh God. They lean back and then lean forward again without falling. I almost kissed the ground. Yes, all the bumping and grinding and walking were worth it. I can't wait to go back.

May 1996

A very long story so it needed its own section. It's section 3—Adam.

June 1998 "Chuckie of Arabia"

I will always be grateful to the internet for giving me the trip of a lifetime. How, you ask? First, I'd had internet in my home in Gaza since 1995. Yes, it was dial-up, and yes it was super slow, but I had it. It was amazing. I could get information about all kinds of things. I fashioned myself the 'queen of the internet search.' I could find anything if given enough time. Mostly I used it to help my students and to satisfy my insatiable curiosity about everything. In about 1996, my mother found email. She was a public-school teacher teaching A.P. English, and the district was implementing this new communication device called email. We had previously been corresponding by snail mail, and while that was fun, email was so much faster, and phone calls back then cost a small fortune when calling overseas.

We could tell each other about our day, what had been happening, what we were doing, etc. My parents came into a windfall and unexpectedly had extra money. I had been extolling the virtues of where I lived on the Mediterranean Sea, and wouldn't they like to come to visit? To my utter shock and delight, they assented to come. And just for good measure, they would bring my mother's younger sister.

This younger sister was not married and didn't have any children, so she was free as a bird. And the thought of actually visiting the places she had only read about as an amateur archaeologist sealed the deal. She was so excited and begged us for a Nile cruise. She'd read all about them and knew that was what she wanted to do.

We would start at Abu Simbel, see the High Aswan Dam, then drive to Luxor, cruise back up the Nile for another six days, and then ride back to Cairo. We saw all the tourist sites, Valley of the Kings, Kom Ombo, The Philae Temple, the Temple of Edfu, the Temple of Horus, the Karnak Temple, the Colossi of Memnon, the Temple of Abydos, and the Luxor Temple. I thought my aunt was going to cry in the Valley of the Kings. She'd dreamed about it longer than I had! At one particular spot, the broken stele, my father was 'kidnapped' by a local merchant. Ok, it was a guy in a souvenir shop who persuaded him to come in to see his wares but kidnapped sounds so much more exciting. He was given tea and shown many items he could take home! They would even ship them even if he chose a large bulky item such as a statue of Ramses for instance. He ended up buying a Felucca, a replica of the boats that locals ply the Nile with. It was a very good thing that it was already put together because my father was about as mechanical as a nail.

One Christmas, I received a bike from Sears that was in a box and needed assembly. I heard words I didn't even know were English that Christmas. I ended up reading the directions to him. That's when we knew who was the mechanical one in the family. It would continue right up until his death. I would come home for a visit, and the VCR would be flashing 12:00 and his digital watch would be off by hours. I would take it from him and in less than a minute, it would be reset until my next visit. The VCR would be reset by guests coming over to visit my brother. Dad always said he and Mom were founders of the Flashing 12 club and that he wasn't on the informational highway (internet), but on a cul de sac.

Dad loved that cruise down the Nile. He was fascinated by the water buffalo as he'd been a dairy farmer and knew the insides and outsides (literally and figuratively) of most breeds of cattle, but these were very new to him. He'd gotten a B.S. in animal husbandry from B.Y.U. mostly in part due to my mother helping him stay focused and study. He wasn't your typical farmer of the day. He was educated and used his knowledge to help his dairy herd produce more milk. I have vivid memories of him 'pulling calves' right out of their mothers, trying to then feed these hungry critters that were as big as I was, and almost getting knocked over. My father would win ribbons for his cows at the state fair, and it was always fun to see them all clean and well-groomed before the 'beauty' contest would begin. But those cows were the bane of my mother's existence. If my father had to go out of town for any reason, the cows somehow knew he was gone, and would leave their field and trundle down the road in front of our house. We got more than one phone call about cows being seen by the neighbor down the street and headed the wrong way. Thank God, they never went the other way as that led to a very busy street with a freeway just beyond that.

I had a swing set in the backyard; ok it was just a piece of land that was between the field and the house. Why wasn't it a backyard? First, Dad never mowed it properly. Second, all the fruit trees and other trees Mom tried to plant would either get knocked over by those roaming herds of cattle, dug up by the roaming pigs, or just die. She gave up after a few years. We had nice evergreen bushes around the house. No one touched the evergreens. They were too boring to bother with! Why did I mention the backyard? Because I have a vivid memory of my father almost crashing through the swing set to get to a cow that had eaten some bad grain and had blown up like a balloon! He screamed for a butcher knife as he only carried a pocket knife. I never saw him without it. He needed a sharp knife to cut the cow open to allow the gas to escape before she killed herself. I have no idea if the cow lived or died. I saw plenty being hauled off in my day. They were picked up by the local supplier to glue and dog food. Yes, they really used parts of dead animals to make Elmer's glue—hence the cow on the label. I couldn't touch glue or paste once I found that out!

Living on that farm taught me many of life's lessons. Birth and death happen all the time. I would lose so many pets that I lost count. Listen to your parents. My father didn't have many rules, but those he did have were set in stone: never go out barefoot, don't play with matches, and never point any gun at another person. So, you guessed it, we broke all of those. I went running out of the house on a nice summer day thinking I'd just run down to the car when I stepped on a steel rake with the tongs pointed up. One of many emergency room visits. I had put only one tong at the base of my toes. Tetanus shot anyone? My brother would also need a run to the E.R. when he tried to peel a carrot with a pocketknife and took off almost a third of the tip of his finger. Before they sewed him up, they put the anesthesia needle right down in the middle of the cut. I almost passed out from just watching, let alone my father or brother.

My brother learned the hard way about not playing with matches. In the milking barn, there was an attic where they stored the grain the cows ate while being milked. If you've ever been in one of those, you know the air is thick with grain particles and it flies everywhere. My brother had gone to the little office that was built to the side of the grain storage area and was trying to light some matches. He couldn't have been five or six at the time, but to this day, he remembers the feel of my father holding his hand over a lit match! My brother could have burned down the whole barn if he'd been outside in that grain dust! And no, I never shot anyone, but I did get a shotgun for my 14th birthday. I took a hunter's safety course and kicked butt on the target shooting. My brother shot out windows and birds with his BB gun but learned how to be safer as he grew older.

The fun thing about living on a farm is the freedom. We could climb and build real forts in the haystack. We skated on frozen cow dung and pee in the winter, got to ride the manure scraper, and hoped we didn't fall off. I learned that dogs really do love cow-toe clippings to chew on. Dad would hire a guy to come over and clip the cows' feet so their hooves wouldn't get too long. I didn't like the de-horning so much. There was burning of the stump on the baby bull's head, but if you didn't do that you'd end up with a bull with horns and that isn't fun to have around. Just ask my uncle! He almost died because Dad's bull didn't like him. Just like chickens, you can't have more than one male around. The bull thought my uncle was too friendly with the ladies and charged him one day. Pinned him against the wall and kept ramming him with those horns. The bull didn't stop until Dad heard the commotion and came out to distract the bull. My uncle ended up with broken ribs and a hurt ego.

Dad may not have been the best farmer ever, or even the luckiest (horse stumbles and falls out of the starting gate at a race, very nice horse founders and dies like the cow in the field from too much grain, horse runs out in a not busy road, but gets hit and dies) but he knew how to handle animals. He could get them to do what he wanted when he wanted it.

As a result, when we got back to Cairo after our little cruise up the Nile, we took a jaunt over to see the pyramids. There were the notorious hawkers of all kinds of souvenirs, but we'd stalked up on our cruise, but Dad couldn't resist the chance to ride a camel. I'd ridden one earlier and didn't wish to repeat the experience, but he wanted to try. The sun was setting, and they put a traditional 'hatta' on him for a picture. You know the checkered Palestinian scarf? Once the camel had stood up, he was something out of a movie: Chuckie of Arabia. None of us knew but he would be dead in six months from an abdominal aortic aneurysm that was misdiagnosed as a repeat kidney stone. I would fly home alone and crying with no arms to run into—see *Adam.* The only bright spot to this terrible loss would be that I got to see my two uncles and my aunt one last time.

My uncle would die from cancer in three months, and I would not be home for my other uncle's passing. My father's funeral had more flowers than the mortuary had ever seen—ever. My father was dearly loved. It was gut-wrenching to see him lying at his viewing and to have to leave him there all alone. I couldn't leave. He'd been such a huge part of who I was. How do you let go of a piece of you? He would be cremated, and his ashes scattered in one of the most remote and most beloved spots for him, the Book Cliffs of southern Utah.

I would stay to help my mother put her shattered life back together. We watched the Super Bowl and tried not to cry too much. Dad loved football. But somehow life goes on. Time doesn't even slow down. Poof, you're gone. What do you have to show for it? Your legacy of good deeds and your good children. I know he has both.

September 1998 Job of a Lifetime

We were perking right along at Palestinian American Language Institute (PALI) and then disaster happened. Amid East, which had been only a testing center for ETS and the TOEFL exam, got permission to be a language center as well as a testing center. Really? We were about to split the not very many students that wanted American English. So, as they say, if you can't beat them, join them. I approached them and said, I'd give up the admin headaches if they'd let me be a head teacher. They enthusiastically agreed. I would go on to become their English Language Teaching Coordinator. I still have my business cards with that title. I have been very lucky in my teaching career to have for the most part not just good jobs, but great jobs. I consider this one of the great jobs.

I got to do something I loved even if the pay wasn't spectacular, the resources sparse (pre-internet), the electricity would go out often which would make watching a video difficult or non-existent. Thank God for batteries because then I could still play the cassette tapes (Google them) for the listening classes. But the students made each and every day worth it. They were sponges trying to soak up each and every bit of information I could give them. As my father told me a long time ago, get paid to do something you love, and you never work a day in your life. He hadn't worked for the last 20 years of his life.

March 1999 Trip of a Lifetime

We were headed to the big city of Dubai, United Arab Emirates. It was so modern and different from Gaza or even Cairo. It was organized. It was clean. It was just like the United States with an Arab twist. I was going there for the TESOL Arabia conference. I was overwhelmed by all the choices of workshops but had learned from a young age to be my own person.

When I was in high school, taking a vocational childcare class, our school was invited to go to Phoenix, Arizona for a conference. Our advisor/teacher didn't find out it was actually an FHA (Future Homemakers of America) conference until we got there. She should have taken the school's officers, but instead had chosen from the various high school classes, and I had been offered the trip. Going to Phoenix from Springville wasn't bad, but by a school bus full of high school girls, it was like herding cats! Once we were there, most of the girls stayed together and took the workshops as a group. I, on the other hand, took whatever they weren't going to. I mean isn't that the point? Get as much information about everything and then share. Not just go en-masse together to every workshop. I remember being curled up on the floor next to the emergency door of the bus and reading the whole way down and back. Ursula Le Guinn can write one mean series and I still love dragons. I was always a rebel of sorts.

Back to Dubai-The most interesting of all was the job fair that was taking place at the same time. I saw hundreds of people lined up to see what postings were being offered. The one with the most buzz was anything to do with the Higher Colleges of Technology (HCT). These are the local colleges that only allow Emiratis to attend free of charge. They are located in each of the seven Emirates and have both a women's and a men's college. They offered a spectacular package including housing, free education for your children, furniture allowance, plus a generous salary. There was only one catch. You had to have your master's degree. Anything less than that and they wouldn't even give you the time of day.

After spending four days in LaLa land, it was hard to come back to reality: grinding poverty, rampant corruption, and harassment from both inside and outside the strip, broken promises, lost dreams. The last one is the hardest to handle. People had such hope and expectation for the future. It just melted away like drifting sand you hardly noticed it till years had passed.

March 1999 Train the Trainer

Being the English Language Teaching Coordinator for Amid East, Gaza, and the West Bank, I was in charge of training the new instructors on what to do. To make me more effective in my training there was a one-week 'Train the Trainer' course being offered in Alexandria. Would I like to go and improve my training skills? Heck ya. Would they pay for my husband to come too? Heck no. I would go by myself to Alexandria as this was company-arranged and paid for. I would later catch up with my husband in Cairo where we then go back to Gaza together. Training was hard as they compressed what usually takes several weeks into one week's worth of training. But I did get to see the modern

Bibliotheca Alexandrina—the new/old library of Alexandria. As one who loves history and reading, this was amazing.

From the glass windows, you looked out onto the harbor where Queen Cleopatra once greeted both Marc Anthony and Julius Caesar. I tried to conjure up an image of the ancient lighthouse but was assaulted by the smells of half-rotten fish and hawkers selling cheap Chinese beach toys. How did we go from such a height in culture and sophistication to such a low point in human history? If you don't believe me, just look at the pictures of the Eid on Alexandria's' beaches. You can't move without stepping or walking over the next person. And the trash piles up so that after three days; you can't stand the smell. What have we done? Burned more than we have read. That's what we've done. I can't imagine what was lost in the great ancient fire. What knowledge, what stories, what history?

I would take all that I had learned from this trip and use it for the rest of my career. I would go on to give many training sessions, and the highest compliment I ever got was that my teachers loved to come to my sessions because they actually learned something useful. I didn't waste their time as so many others had. They got information they could use and apply right away in their own classrooms. Isn't that the object of teaching? To give information that someone can use?

May 1999 The President Will See You Now

Since I had met my husband, he'd been very active and athletic. We even took a golf course together for a college P.E. credit. We joined an athletic club and he wanted to learn how to play tennis, so he took a couple of lessons from the local pro. How much that would change his life, we couldn't have guessed. He was a natural. He was good at it. He loved it! It would hurt him physically, and he would need at least four surgeries to repair torn pieces from playing the sport he loved too much. He would go on to be the Palestinian National Tennis champion three years in a row: 1994, 1995, and 1996. He would serve as the Vice President of the Palestinian National Tennis Association all the time we lived in Gaza. He would be a USPTA-certified coach level 2. No small feat. Do you get that he loved tennis—with all his heart?

When we arrived back in 1993, there was only one tennis court in the whole of the Gaza Strip. He would refurbish one and was trying to build more. Because of Oslo, and because of a close personal connection to Yasser Arafat's personal representative, he was able to make relationships with the Israeli Tennis Association. They furnished him with blueprints and plans of their national tennis center and he had the grand idea to build one in Gaza. He had the land given to him, but now he needed to find the funding to build the stadium and practice courts. There wasn't any money in Gaza, so he looked to the United States. He even traveled at his own expense and went on a pledge tour for two weeks trying to drum up support for a National Tennis Complex. He even met with some wealthy Jews for Peace to help out. There are some very generous Palestinians living and working in the United States. For the right cause, they would give liberally by pledging to donate the money. Now he only needed to find someone as passionate about tennis as he was. Would you believe he found such a person? And this person was not just willing to pledge but would even fly to Gaza at his own personal expense to seal the deal. There was just one catch. Isn't there always? He wanted to meet President Yasser Arafat personally. No problem. Because of the connection with the personal representative, the meeting would happen.

Did I mention that the personal representative to Arafat played tennis? And really liked my husband? And had taken my husband to see the tennis centers in Israel in his own personal car? So, he was very involved and wanted to make this deal happen.

We knew the morning of the expected visit, but not the exact time as the president's schedule was very fluid. My husband had arranged to pick up the VIP visitor and take him to the presidential compound on the beach. I got a phone call about half an hour later asking how soon could I be ready. Ready for what? I could come along to the visit if I so desired. What? An opportunity to meet any president was way too exciting. Actually, I'm glad I didn't know about it beforehand. If I had, I would have been way too nervous to even move. As it was, I'm sure I ran around like a chicken with my head cut off. What do you wear to meet a president? I threw on my best dress and hoped for the best.

We, my husband, myself, and the VIP, were ushered into a sitting area where we met the president, Yasser Arafat. He grabbed my hand and kissed it like the Europeans do. My husband was just hoping he would stop there which he did. And after everyone shook everyone's hand, all the ministers, and advisors, we were then ushered into a long room with a very long table. I thought we were just going to get the meet-and-greet photo op, but actually, we were invited to share their lunch.

The president indicated that I would be seated to his right as he sat at the head of the table, and the VIP would be on my right with my husband to his right. We both looked at each other and shrugged. What can you do when the president himself has told you where to sit? I could hardly breathe, let alone eat! But there was fresh fish and all the side dishes. Actually, the president ate soup and salad. He didn't eat the fried fish. I was told later that that was his normal diet, in reality quite plain and simple.

My Arabic wasn't very good, but I could pick up bits and pieces of the conversation around the table. It mainly focused on whether the grapes in the West Bank were better than the grapes grown in the sandy soil near the beach in Gaza. Trust me they aren't. But there was a lively debate raging as some members of the group were from the West Bank and defended their grapes as if they were their children.

When the meal was over, the servers brought out large trays of fruit. This is the Arab idea of dessert. The president must have liked watermelon because there was a large tray of it placed right in front of him. I don't like watermelon. I don't like most fruit, but I really don't like watermelon. So of course, what happened? The president himself put a couple of pieces of the offending fruit on my plate. What could I do? I ate it of course. When I was done, he put more pieces on my plate. My husband would later recount the story saying I had eaten more watermelon that day than I had for the last five years!

Thank God, we were done with lunch and now retired to the photo room. The room with the plush cross-stitch chairs and flags. The room where everyone gets their photo taken.

But before we actually left the table, the president flagged an aide and whispered into his ear. Wow, state secrets right in front of me! I was standing to the side politely waiting my turn while the VIP got all the photos, he needed to be happy and write that fat check. Then the aide who the president had whispered to appeared with a Bedouin cross-stitch jacket. If you've never seen the Bedouin cross-stitch, it is something to admire. Very small cross stitches in mostly red that stretch up and down long dresses of black or white. It takes hundreds of hours to make a dress let alone a jacket that was solid in red cross-stitch! Yes, I said solid, front and back. I'm a bit naive, and I thought they wanted me to 'dress up' for the photo.

My husband corrected my mistake and told me that actually, the president was giving me the jacket and a scarf (with the same cross-stitch) to go with it. I would meet several women who either got a scarf or a jacket, but none who got both! I was in so much shock that I almost missed the part where the president held the jacket so I could wear it! What a gentleman! I think I actually floated home. I wear it proudly to events and dinners and tell the lunch story to go along with it. It will be a family heirloom for my only daughter. It is with such sadness that I report that the tennis center was never actually built. It broke my husband's heart but not his spirit for tennis or the Palestinian cause. There is a park where it would have been if that's any consolation. My husband refurbished a couple of tennis courts over the years and still loves to play with his tennis buddies.

September 1999 Cruising Is the Only Way to Travel

I have loved cruising since I took my first cruise back in 1988. It was a short three-day cruise around Santa Catalina Island just off of Los Angeles, but it got me hooked. We had been living in my husband's home country on visit visas for the past six years. It wasn't easy, but in the beginning, we could renew our 'six-month visa' by sending it in so that meant we had a year. Then they moved it to every three months, but we could still send them in for renewal. We needed to renew yet again our 'visit visa' and coincidentally there was a cruise leaving Haifa. We contacted the travel agent; gave him our information and we were booked! It wasn't the best cruise I've ever had, but it wasn't the worst either. The entire crew was Russian. I have nothing against Russians, but their English had a lot to be desired. From the look on the passenger's faces, so did their Hebrew.

The absolute best cruise I've ever been on was the Eastern Mediterranean seven-day cruise. It didn't start off that way. This is the cruise I had been dreaming about my whole life. We would be going to Crete, Santorini, Rhodes, and Ephesus in Turkey. I was so excited and couldn't believe I was going. When we landed in Athens, we thought that the ship would leave at 5:00. That was the time written on the itinerary I had printed off our reservation. We decided to take the public bus to the port as a taxi sounded way too expensive and we had time. When we got off the bus at what we thought looked like the port, we were in fact on the wrong side of the port.

The cruise ship was way on the other side. Again, we didn't take a taxi, but decided to walk, dragging our luggage as we went along. At least we hoped it was our cruise ship. We came around the corner, and sure enough, it was our ship. But would you believe, as we walked up to it, it was pulling away from the dock! Are you kidding? My dream cruise is leaving without me. No, this can't be happening! I looked at my husband, and if looks could kill, he would have been dead a thousand times over! I was hysterical and inconsolable by now. The cruise people were quite used to this and just let me carry on. My husband was actually quite calm and kept trying to reassure me that my dream had not just floated away on the boat. Once I could breathe with some normalcy, they gave us our options. There was no option of rebooking. They would 'hold' our cabin and keep it for us. What do you mean 'hold' it? They went on to explain that there was a flight from Athens to Crete where to ship would be two days from now! Did they just say two days? Yes, it would take the cruise two days to get to Crete where we could meet up with it and board and then continue on our merry way.

So, what to do in Athens? Hm…Well, I've heard that there was this large building that was absolutely ancient and maybe worth seeing. Are you kidding? We jumped at the chance to stay in a modest hotel just below the Parthenon. Yes, the Parthenon! By the time we'd checked in and made sure we knew how and when to get to the airport, we had about a day and a half to kill. We were hungry and decided to find a restaurant. We walked up behind our hotel on a path not wide enough for one car to go down and were surprised by all the people walking. We walked for a bit and saw a restaurant with a menu for you to peruse before entering. It looked quaint and the host took us up a flight of stairs. We came upon the second floor which was busy and that is always a good sign. If locals eat at a place, then it's pretty safe for tourists. He asked if we would prefer their balcony. What balcony? I saw a little platform as wide as the chair with another chair across from the smallest table possible. I've seen end tables bigger!

But once we sat down, the view was breathtaking. By now it was getting dark, and the Acropolis had been lit up! Just like the postcards show! It was one of the most romantic dinners I've ever had. I couldn't tell you the food we ordered. Who cared? It was straight out of a movie. We explored around us a bit more, but I guarantee, missing the boat was the best thing to ever happen to us.

I woke up to the Parthenon out my window. We walked up and down it, and still had another half day. We chose to walk to the Athens Museum which wasn't that far away. I can't begin to explain how fascinating it was. It is built over excavations that they are still working on. To climb up and actually see the Elgin Marbles, OK only those that the English didn't steal, was spectacular. They have the originals in place, with the missing pieces filled in, but in plaster and very white. You can tell what's missing. But it's still a marvel. I was standing in front of a statue and heard a woman telling some tourists what the statue was and where they had found it. I knew my Greek Gods and Goddesses (think teaching those last semester students at the Islamic University) and was listening intently. When the couple had had their fill, the woman turned to us and asked if we had any questions.

Any questions? Are you kidding? I wanted to know the entire Greek history. It turned out she was a docent and had a Ph.D. in archaeology no less. We kept her for over an hour questioning everything we saw. She was so patient and didn't rush us at all. I think she was very pleased to have someone who was genuinely interested and knowledgeable. We had such a nice time. It was a spectacular day. And then we had another romantic evening. We took a plane the next day and the cruise ship wasn't even there yet. They would take another day to get to Crete! We stayed in another hotel on the beach and spent the evening walking along the shore and trying to decide which of the many fish restaurants we would visit. We woke to an incredible sunrise I'll never forget, and the ship was there too! We calmly made our way to the ship while most people were getting off to spend the day exploring the island. We settled into our cabin and then had a few hours to kill, so yes let's explore the island more. Then we finally got to 'cruise' to the next island.

Rhodes was not what I expected, mostly crusader castle buildings. Santorini would literally take our breath away. We took the cable car up, and walked down, not wanting to ride the poor little donkeys pressed into service of fat tourists. This is one place I know we'll go back to.

I'd been to Turkey but only Anatolia and it was a day trip on another cruise. I would be blown away by Ephesus. The scale and the size can't be imagined. You have to walk all over it to really understand the magnitude. Yes, we saw the public toilets still in situ. But the amphitheater and shops were actually much more interesting. You could just feel the bustle and bump—that was because it was so crowded. That wasn't hard to imagine. If you lost sight of your guide, you'd really be lost.

The best part and what made it so worth the heartache of missing the boat was that by the time we docked, got off the ship, and drove to the airport (in a bus), we wouldn't have had time or energy to visit the Acropolis or the museum! I got more than my trip of a lifetime and didn't spend two days at sea with nothing to see. I saw Athens in the best and most romantic way.

It was the cruise of a lifetime, a lifetime ago. But back to our 'Russian' cruise. We visited Cyprus again. It wasn't very memorable except when we actually left the boat at the end. We were stopped by passport control. Where were we headed? We didn't lie, we said Gaza, and not only that, but we had purchased a T.V. in the duty-free shop. You should have seen the officer's face. He turned six shades of red. How did we get on board? We explained that we bought a ticket just like everyone else. He was flabbergasted. They couldn't send us back. Back to where? This was our point of origin. We would find out later that we couldn't even travel out of Ben Gurion Airport anymore and that the last time we tried, they had arrested my husband and wanted to send him back. See Czech Republic below. So, in the end, they had to let us in, and with our brand new T.V., no less.

June 2000 How Did You?

It was getting harder and harder to leave to renew visas. Where to go? We'd been all over the neighboring places. I was almost sick of Cairo. Ok not really, but I wanted something different. Some place we'd never been. We got a crazy idea to go to Eilat by bus no less, and then cross over to Taba, Egypt. Sure, no problem. The border guard was freaked out. How did we get on the bus? From where? And now what? Send us back by bus? Detain us—for riding a bus? She kept us for a couple of hours and then released us. We ended up in Sharm El Sheik. Not a bad place to end up if you have to go to Egypt! The beaches are some of the best in the world.

28 September 2000 The Day the Peace Died

'Peace' hadn't turned out to be exactly like everyone thought it would. There had been such hope in the air in Gaza when Arafat had returned, but that had disappeared like morning fog and left only poverty, despair, and broken dreams. When you have nothing left to live for, you look for a good way to die. When Arial Sharon visited the Harem Al Shariff, he knew exactly what he was doing. He was a military leader, and he wanted an excuse to let loose the dogs of war! He would never know how much it would cost both sides.

30 September 2000, I Can't Watch It Again

Mohammed Durra was only 12 years old. He had his whole life ahead of him. Even his own father couldn't keep him safe from bullets. He died in a hail of gunfire. Israeli soldiers admitted they had killed the innocent bystander but would later dispute the claim of murder in cold blood. My problem was the T.V. was showing him being murdered, over and over again and again. A passing film crew caught the whole bloody thing on tape and news outlets wouldn't stop showing it over, and over. Mohammed was only one of eight killed in the first three days of Intifada number 2.

I personally knew people who left within days of the start of the Intifada. I guess we stayed because we had nothing to go back to and we didn't imagine that it would last for years only to dissolve into a full-scale war years later.

May 2001 Too Close for Comfort

They actually did it. The Israeli army had used an F-16 and actually blew up Yasser Arafat's personal helicopter only a couple of blocks from our house. I was hysterical. If they could do that, they could blow up any building, with anyone in it and they would go on to do this. I knew we wouldn't be a target, at least that's what I kept telling myself.

November 2001 But I'm Worried About You!

We needed to renew our visas yet again. It was becoming slightly ridiculous. Now it was cut down to every three months. It had been every six months, but you could ask to renew it and theoretically stretch it to a year before needing to actually leave and return. Now it was every three months, no exceptions. If you didn't have a valid visa when you left, they could theoretically prevent you from entering for five years! Being forced to travel isn't as nice as it sounds. Leaving your job, your kids, your comfort. And you must pay for this pleasure. And they make you pay for leaving and coming! It was getting expensive. But we tried to make the most of it. Where should we go now? Why not the Czech Republic? They weren't communists anymore. They were close. And most of all they were cheap!

Despite not speaking any Czech, we managed with English and sign language. We even booked a day tour that was quite enlightening. We learned all about Czech crystal, and even drank the invigorating waters at a very old 'spa.' The tour guide was quite despondent at showing us a church that had been desecrated and destroyed by invaders. She hinted that they were definitely not Christians and looked at us. We'd told her where we were from, but she was still informative if not a bit cool. She took us to the National Museum. She was so proud of it. Having been in a couple of museums myself, and even been a docent once, I was not so much impressed. Their idea of what and how it should be displayed left a lot to be desired. But at least they were trying.

While you are a tourist, you need to 'get lost.' Just wander and you will discover things you never even knew existed. I found the Trevi fountain that way. Just wandering the streets of Rome, and suddenly we were there. I was shouting and running, and my husband thought I had gone crazy! When we wandered up the hill to see the Citadel in Petra, we discovered the Lion Fountain and the most ancient seller. We love to wander.

Hence, we wandered in Prague. We found the ancient bridge—the Charles Bridge started in 1357. We actually, by accident, found the Prague Astronomical Clock—installed in 1410. We were wandering in history. It was magical. And for fun, we decided to hop on a metro. That's the fun thing about maps. You don't need to be able to read any language.

They are like ancient pictographs. You just follow the colored lines.

I remember calling my mother from a pay phone to check on her. It had only been a couple of months post 9/11 and I wanted to be sure she was safe. At that time, we weren't sure there wouldn't be other attacks. The irony that I'm worried about her being attacked is not lost on me.

This would be a most memorable trip for another reason. Upon arrival at Ben Gurion Airport, where we had been leaving from for the past seven years, was suddenly and without warning a no-go zone. They arrested my husband and wanted to put him back on the plane to the Czech Republic. What? Are you crazy? He's not from there, we live here, and he's an American Citizen. You can't just arrest him for flying! Oh yes, they can. I tried calling the American Embassy and got a recording that they were closed. Closed? How does an embassy close? I needed them now! No help there as usual. He finally got the guard to let him talk to me on a house phone at the airport and my husband explained to me that in fact, they couldn't just ship him back because the Czech Republic had no reason to accept him. He wasn't their citizen. Thank God.

On his way back to the holding cell, he had noticed that the guard was watching an NBA game. It just so happened that my husband was wearing a Utah Jazz basketball team shirt. So, he spent the next hour or so watching the game with the guard until the guard got nervous about someone catching my husband out of the cell. Next, they would just hold him long enough to collect enough men to fill a taxi to Gaza. And furthermore, I should find a taxi and go home by myself. By myself? Are you nuts? God, I hate traveling alone—after my father passed, *Adam*. This was becoming a habit I did not want to continue.

He actually followed me by a little more than a couple of hours, but I didn't know that at the time. This was not when everyone had a cell phone. It would be the last time we'd fly out of that airport. It was the last time any Palestinian who didn't have great influence would fly out of there. Now the only way in or out was land borders with Egypt or Jordan. Neither of these were exactly friendly toward Palestinians.

29 March 2002 Birthplace of the King of Peace

Palestinian Authority headquarters were under such heavy attack and in fact, the compound in Ramallah was 75% destroyed. My husband's uncle was a lieutenant colonel in the Palestinian Authority military. He was with Arafat when this was happening and made one of the most dramatic and scary phone calls I've ever heard. He was saying goodbye to the family. He thought his life was over and they would finish off the rest of the compound. They didn't. In fact, the uncle was tasked with negotiating with the Israelis to halt the standoff at the Church of the Nativity in Bethlehem (where Christians believe Christ was born). What most people don't know is that to get physically into the church, you must duck and crouch to then pass in. It was built like that to keep out horseback riders. How do I know this?

I've visited it a couple of times, but the first was in 1984. I'd just found out that I was pregnant, and we'd gone away for a trip to see Jerusalem and Bethlehem. During that first visit, it occurred to me that it was ironic that I was pregnant, and we couldn't find a hotel to stay in. We kept walking and walking and every time, they were full up! The irony was not lost on me.

The standoff in the church ended with a settlement that the uncle had personally negotiated, and no one was shot coming out. The church had been full of Palestinians seeking refuge from a hail of bullets by the Israeli soldiers. There are still some sacred sites left in the world.

I think that was the last proverbial straw for me. If a lieutenant colonel couldn't keep himself safe and sound, how could we civilians ever hope to cope? People were dying all around us. Incursions by Israeli forces were a daily occurrence. Young men were being sniped on their rooftops just for looking over. I was worried and scared. Not a good combination. I had two, not one, but two teenage boys. I had a choice. I could get us out. I was a mother on a mission.

Believe me, it wasn't that easy. Three children in school and finals coming up. You want what? To take the finals before they are even prepared? Impossible. I'm the queen of the impossible (see *Adam*). We arranged for the exams and to get their school certificates stamped and certified so they could go on to the next grade. Take that impossible!

May 2002 Who Said You Can't Go Home?

We were home. Ok, it was home for me. It was the house where my father had died. It was full of many childhood memories for me. It was safe and warm. My oldest son would go to my high school in the fall and attend his last year of school. My second son would be entering high school and my daughter would be in middle school. Another irony was my baby would end up taking ESL for his first year of school. Yes, you read correctly, he'd gotten so good at Arabic that his English was not up to par.

May 2003 No Regrets—Ever

Life has a funny way of going on with or without you. We had settled into a comfortable routine and of course, we missed our family in Gaza too much. The house phone rang, and the person asked for my son. That was a bit odd, but he had been making friends. My son just kept saying yes and then turned ash colored. He looked so upset that by the time he hung up the phone, I knew something was terribly wrong. He told us that his very best friend had just been killed by Israeli soldiers. The friend had been studying for his final year exams on his own roof. My mind raced and said a prayer as my son could have been with him and killed or seen it happen. And then be expected to take his exams that would determine the rest of his life? No. Thank God. I have never ever regretted leaving. I gave our family a chance. Too many haven't had that chance.

Random Thoughts: Jerusalem

It is a city of wonder, smells, and sights, but mostly people. The old city is amazing and one of my favorite places. Yes, there are places to worship—Al Aqsa Mosque with its burnt door still on display, The Dome of the Rock—with its hidden underground grotto, and the Church of the Holy Sepulchre—with a Muslim doorkeeper. But it is the people that make the city so wonderful and inviting. I love wandering around the 'Christian' quarter. It is full of mother-of-pearl items and so many leather products. The smell is overwhelming. As you keep going the sights and smells almost overpower you, but you recover as you stop and look at something that has caught your eye. Then you are assaulted by the smell of fresh meat. It's just hanging there. No wondering which cut of meat you got. You can pick it yourself off the carcass. One of the treats though is from the cart sellers who offer boiled eggs and local bread—kaik. Crusty on the outside, and light and fluffy on the inside, it's great for dipping into olive oil or zaatar (ground up thyme). I loved wandering the 'streets.'

Gaza Souks

I loved just meandering around the open-air markets that can be found throughout the Gaza Strip. Each area has its own particular smell, feel, and noise. Some are just for clothing and the clothes are hanging from the rooftops all around you. You are bombarded by the colors and textures. Then there are the food areas. It is hard to explain the assault on your senses. Colors from the spices, aromas from the meat, and produce that are left lying around. Sounds of the chickens, ducks, and even turkeys that are for sale and they can kill it and send you on your way with a fresh animal for dinner. I loved buying from the older ladies selling vegetables and fruits. They have the years etched on their faces from years in the sun, just like farmers back home. I also enjoyed the junkyard areas. You could find a part for almost anything…a broken mixer, a broken vacuum, a broken T.V. They could fix anything. And I do mean anything. They had to. There were no spare parts. You either had to cannibalize or find a way to fix it. Mostly, they fixed it. Even now, they are using the leftover pipes that brought water to the settlements in the middle of the Gaza Strip to make rockets! A nice circle of life if you ask me.

Part 3
Adam

I should have died at least half a dozen times before now. I shouldn't be alive. Yet here I am writing about all this. I know you're probably wondering how does this relate to 'Adam.' But trust me, you will see the connection.

September 1962

I should start at the beginning, at least my beginning. I was born full-term on Labor Day. There was only one problem—I was born with pneumonia. This is number one. How does one get born with full-blown pneumonia? The doctors had no idea. So instead of taking me home, my mother had to leave me in the PICU (which they didn't really have by the way), so just a regular hospital crib with an oxygen tent over the crib. I got massive doses of Tetracycline which would permanently gray my teeth (and which can't be fixed by Zoom or any other whitening product—only veneers) but saved my life. Imagine wanting to hold and cuddle your newborn, but only for a few minutes each day. My mother told me I would be lying on the crib lifeless and motionless until I caught sight of her, and I would perk up and squeal and move around. My mother was in her second to last term of her bachelor's degree. The next term would be student teaching.

November 1962

I finally get to go home. My parents were living in a cockroach-infested basement apartment close to the university where my mother and father were studying. Here comes number two. I was only a couple of months old when my parents were sleeping and heard a loud bang in the morning. They awoke to find their apartment filled with black dust everywhere. The oil radiator heating unit had exploded and burst with black dust covering everything in the living room. This included me. My mother tells of running into the living room and seeing nothing but black everywhere. She was convinced that I was dead as I had been sleeping in a crib in the living room. But then I opened my eyes. I was alive only to face a much bigger threat.

March 1963

When I was about six months old, my mother was facing her final term at university—student teaching. If you've ever done this, then you know it is one of the hardest things to do—face teenagers and expect them to follow your orders. No teenager willingly does what you tell them to do, so it is a daunting challenge and one you need all your wits about you, not a sickly crying baby. My paternal grandmother volunteered to take me in for a while. I think my mother was relieved and sad at the same time. Happy that she could focus on her student teaching, sad that I was over four hours away by car in the little town of Jerome, Idaho.

Since my paternal grandmother died of cancer when I was six, all that I know is what I've been told by my mother. But evidently, I started to cough and choke while she was babysitting me. Not just the little cough when a baby gets a tickle in the throat, but I was choking and couldn't catch my breath. I was turning blue. I must have been very bad because my grandmother actually baptized me as Catholic as she thought I was about to die on her. I rallied, but just barely. She, of course, rushed me to the hospital, and my maternal grandmother (who was an LPN) got me admitted. Of course, the first thing they did was a barium x-ray. This was the early 1960s. Long before there were ultrasound or CT or MRI's available like now. They did what they had. Then they freaked out. I actually had barium in my lungs. It turns white on the x-ray film so there isn't any mistaking it for something else. I had it in my lungs. How was that even possible as it is supposed to be only in my stomach?

I had a fistula. A hole that actually formed a tube (connection) between my esophagus and my trachea. But I get ahead of myself. First, I had to have the surgery to confirm this. But it was the doctors' golfing day—Wednesday. It must have been March or April as I was born in September. The only surgeon was out on the golf course and couldn't be bothered. Thank God for strong grandmas. Both of mine chased him out on the golf course and when he wasn't amenable to coming in for my surgery, let's just say my two grandmas convinced him otherwise. I've heard one actually grabbed a golf ball and threatened to use it as a weapon, but that can't be confirmed.

I was in the hospital in Twin Falls, Idaho. I had a reluctant surgeon, but a great family to support me. I was put on a breathing machine (intubated) and they started to cut me open on my back left shoulder along the shoulder blade. I coughed up the breathing tube. How is that even possible? Near-death number three. The surgeon came out and told my mother, as by now she had driven like a madman the four hours to get there, that if I'd done that while they had my chest cavity open, I would have died as they didn't have a smaller tube and no way to put it back in. Oh, they didn't have a smaller tube? Really? And you thought it would work?

Remember the next part, please.

I was driven by ambulance from Twin Falls, Idaho, to LDS Hospital in Salt Lake City, Utah. They had a smaller tube. The downside was they decided to go in on my right shoulder to crack it open and get to the fistula. The doctor would later tell my mother that my 'connection' was almost completely horizontal if not slightly tilted up. If it had been tilted down, I would have drowned a long time ago. Remember the pneumonia at birth? Yes, this was a direct cause of that as the moisture collected in this tube, then ran down into my lungs. Remember the barium? Same thing. Great. I'm fixed. I go home and recover with a short scar on my left shoulder, and a longer one on my right that goes from the top of my shoulder, down and around to into my right breast. It would make wearing a swimsuit a nightmare, but I was alive.

September 1963

At about a year old, I was coughing and choking again! Not again. Yes again. My parents were still making payments on the first surgery when I needed another one. Would you believe barium in the lungs again? Yes, it was true. And yes, they found another fistula an inch below the first one. So, I made medical history—two H fistulas and I was alive. This was number four. The only really disappointing thing about the second surgery was that they went in on my right side again. It made an already big scar, much bigger and wider. I hated it as a teenager but wore it as a badge of honor later in life. My parents were forgiven for the second surgery. I would be six years old before they paid off the first surgery. It was kind of a buy-one-get-one-free situation.

Somewhere between the first and second surgery was number five. My mother was driving her car when she took a railroad track crossing faster than was completely safe. For her and the car, it wasn't a big deal. But for me, the passenger, riding in of all things a bathtub, not tied down in any fashion by the way, I ended up face down on the passenger side floor with the tub on top of me. Thank God, we have car seats now that survive almost any impact!

November 1963

Sometime shortly after my second surgery, came number six. My parents loved the outdoors and went camping up in the mountains above our home. They had a tent and camp stools. I was sitting on a camp stool in front of the campfire when I flopped off the chair and into the fire. My mother swears she has never moved so fast in her life. She had me out of the fire and dusted off before my father could even react. It was so fast; I didn't have any burns let alone scars. I had enough of those, I guess.

I could list the time I fell off a galloping horse in our field, the time I was kicked in the shin by my dad's horse, or even the time Dad thought he had run me over with the truck. But as I said in the beginning, there were around a half dozen times, and I need to go on with the story.

May 1996

It was a bright Tuesday morning. I had taken my three children to school and came back to have breakfast like any other day. My back hurt but being nine months pregnant can do that to a person. I had a doctor's appointment for the next day with my OB/GYN. I liked my doctor. He spoke English. He had studied in England, and he promised me an epidural. With three previous pregnancies in the States, and all three having epidurals, it was one of two things I had requested. I had also requested that my husband be in the delivery room with me. As far as we know, he's the only man to be in with his wife as we've never heard of it before or since. It was something completely out of the ordinary as the Dr. said he'd never heard of it in Gaza. I had no qualms about having number four. I had done this before and knew what to expect. Or so I thought. How dumb was that thought?

Nothing about this birth was anything like the other three. First, I was in Gaza, Palestine. Second, I would end up in the 'English Hospital' with equipment that looked right out of the dark ages. Third, I wouldn't get that sought-after epidural after all because the back ache turned into contractions. The contractions would force me to call the doctor and meet him at the hospital.

Here's the good news—I was dilated to an eight. The bad news is that I was too far gone to have an epidural. And then worse news—my contractions stopped. Are you kidding? What do we do now? The international standby, Pitocin. So, as any pregnant woman who has been given Pitocin can testify, it started my contractions again, but with unnatural force.

I can honestly say I thought I was dying for about five minutes. I had been manhandled and forced to actually walk over to the delivery chair. So much for five-star service. I don't remember having to do that in the States. But again, I wasn't in the States. I was in Gaza. I was lucky to have a private room where I could scream like a banshee. Yes, I am a screamer. Remember, I thought I was dying. I thought my body was being torn into two pieces. That's what it felt like. Damn, I wanted an epidural for a reason.

Then I was flooded with all the hormones I could handle. What pain? What screaming? I had a perfect little boy with ten fingers and ten toes. What could possibly be wrong? He was breathing; I didn't even have to have any stitches. Remember this was child number four. Oh, how wrong could I have been?

The OB/GYN took about one minute and ordered my husband to take my brand-new born son to the children's hospital immediately. What in the world? I was recovering in a side room, and vaguely remember being told to take a taxi home and meet them at the house. We weren't given any instructions or what he suspected. Sometimes, ignorance is bliss. Sometimes it isn't. Trust me, on this one it wasn't.

Miraculously, we met at the house at about the same time. We walked up the stairs together. Everyone greeted us and wanted to see the newest addition to the growing family. Because I had married the oldest son, our children were some of the first of dozens to be added later. Naming our third son wasn't hard. I had always liked the name Adam, as it worked in English as well as Arabic. It was a traditional name for a very untraditional boy.

Of course, I had all the nursery trappings ready for a newborn. I had done this three times before. This wasn't my first rodeo. I had nursed the others and had no compunction about nursing number four. He latched on and at first seemed to enjoy nursing. But almost immediately I knew something wasn't right. He was bubbling at the mouth. You read that correctly. Bubbling. It reminded me of when you blow through a straw into a glass of milk, and it foams up. He looked like that. What? How could that possibly be? Then he started to choke a little. I had to get the foam out of the way, but how? I had brought a few items with me, and I remembered the bulb syringe that I had from my previous babies. You should use it to suck out mucus from the baby's nose, but I needed it and I needed it now. He was a bit fussy, but he was a newborn baby. That was to be expected. Then I noticed something that really made me scared.

His skin had started to look strange. It didn't look plump and soft. It looked dry and brittle. In fact, when I grabbed it, it stayed pinched. That is a clear indication of dehydration (years of working in a hospital as a floating clerk, you pick up a few things along the way). How could he be dehydrated? I was nursing him every hour or so.

By midnight, the bubbles were much worse, and he was really choking now. His skin was really bad now. I had no clue as to what was going on, only that he needed medical attention and he needed it now. We three (my husband, the baby, and I) drove to the children's hospital.

When we got there, they could see the baby was in distress, but there weren't any doctors, and hardly any nurses. Yes, you read correctly, no doctors. How do I know there weren't any nurses? Because I had to suction the baby throughout the night. Yes, me. Who had just given birth, and hadn't had a minute of rest since getting home?

I was given a crib in a baby ward with three other children. I was told, "Here is the suction device, and you use it thus." I was at least given a chair. So, there I am, from midnight until six a.m. getting up every ten minutes or so to suction my brand newborn baby boy. I'm not even sure if he had an I.V. or not at that point in time.

Why do I know the time exactly? Because the 'cleaning crew' (who were actually the mothers of the sick children) insisted that the floor needed to be cleaned at this time. They acted as if this was the routine. Up at six to clean the floor and wait for the doctors to arrive anytime from seven to eight o'clock.

We had called my husband's second cousin on his father's side, as he was a pediatrician. We informed him of the trip to the hospital right after our son had been born but knew nothing of why or what was or wasn't found during that trip. We would later learn that the x-ray technician had made a critical mistake that nearly cost our son his life.

The x-ray the technician botched was again performed that morning correctly. My OB/GYN had suspected something was greatly wrong when I presented with way too much amniotic fluid. Way more than normal. How could that be? The x-ray tech had passed a wire down into my son's lungs, not his stomach like he was supposed to. How do we know? Because that morning when it was done correctly, the wire couldn't go down to the stomach because his esophagus stopped in a blind pouch. We learned later that his stomach was actually connected to his lungs!

I later learned that in utero, babies actually drink amniotic fluid. Babies actually pee and drink it as well. Fascinating, but what do we do now? I remember sitting outside the hospital, we had a nurse to watch him as it was daytime, and just crying in disbelief, actually weeping in despair. I went through the gamut of emotions—horrified, scared, sad, mad, and guilty. After all, I had had esophageal trouble at birth as well. But we had to do something and do it now.

We were transferred to Shifa Hospital (the site of the beginning of the first Intifada) by ambulance in hopes that we could connect with a surgeon and fix my son. At least that was the plan. Shifa was the only place to have surgery in the whole Gaza Strip.

We arrived in Shifa only to find out that the surgeon was on vacation but may come to the hospital today. What do you mean may come to the hospital later in the day? My son needed surgery now! We managed to catch up with the surgeon. The hospital had called him and mentioned our case. He was, of course, sympathetic and told us we had three choices. Choice number one was to let him do the surgery in Shifa Hospital. He was familiar with the surgery and had studied how to perform it. It was pretty straightforward—disconnect the stomach from the lungs (closing the hole), open the closed esophagus, and then connect the stomach to the esophagus. Easy-peasy.

There was only one problem. My son was less than a day old. The smallest ventilator they had was for a child, not a newborn infant. Even if they had a machine they could adapt, they didn't have the staff to monitor or care for him. Not so easy now. So, what was choice number two? Take him by ambulance and hope he doesn't die on the way there to the hospital in Jerusalem. Yes, they could probably do the surgery, and they probably had post-surgical care, but they weren't the best. Hence, choice number three.

Assaf Harofeh-Ramlah (30 minutes outside Tel Aviv). They had not only the staff and a Newborn Intensive Care Unit (NICU), but they had the best surgeon in all of Europe. Babies were flown in from as far away as Russia, just to be operated on by this surgeon. How did a doctor in Gaza know all this? He had learned how to do the surgery from this expert. He even called him for us. Now we only had the monumental task of getting not just an ambulance, but a driver and a doctor as well as a newborn baby with no identity papers all the way to the middle of Israel from Gaza, Palestine.

The timing of this couldn't have been worse. This was May 1996. There had just been a terrible attack on a bus in Tel Aviv in April with multiple deaths. Netanyahu had been running for the office of prime minister and was about to win the first time. He ran on a platform of getting tough on Palestinians. It wasn't a good time to be a Palestinian trying to get into Israel. It would, of course, get a lot worse, but for the time being, it was hard enough.

While my husband was trying to arrange this monumental task, I was waiting in a pediatric room in Shifa with my son. He was on an I.V. by now but wasn't getting much better. We would later learn that he had pneumonia because of the negative pressure created by having his stomach connected to his lungs. It was literally sucking stomach juices (acid) into his lungs. This would be a complication later on, but we didn't know this at the time. The room we were in was again a four-crib unit with mothers sitting next to their sick children.

At one point, we were shown a few rooms away, a mother sitting with her child in a crib. We were told that the child was 'waiting' for the same surgery my son needed. The doctor told us that about one baby a month is born with this variant of birth defects. She was facing the same difficulties we were, but my son had me and my husband. There was no way we were going to just sit by and watch him die. Not if I had one breath of life left in me.

Remember what I said about my son laying in a crib? He started to cough and choke. Does this sound familiar? He actually turned blue. I had heard my whole life that I had turned blue and that's why my grandmother had baptized me. I could have gone forever, not knowing what that looked like, but here I was facing it. I started to scream for help. A female nurse heard me and came running into the room. I was not hysterical until she started screaming. She was screaming for help! That's when I lost it. I started screaming, in English mind you, and my father-in-law came running to see what all the noise was about. Then he started shouting for help in Arabic.

A male nurse heard the noise and came in. He took one look at the fixtures on the wall above the crib and took off out the door. I ran after him. He had run into the next room and was scanning the fixtures in this room. I had no idea what he was looking for, but he knew it when he found it. His adrenaline must have been pumping because he took the oxygen hose off the wall fixture with one arm pull. I had worked in a hospital for over five years, and I knew what it took to put on and take off a hose connected to the wall. The male nurse then ran back to my son's crib and jammed the hose onto the wall fixture, again with one movement. He then turned on the oxygen and revived my son. Obviously, by now, I was shaking and in hysterics. My son was dying right before my eyes.

My father-in-law, once he knew my son would be ok, went to find my husband. I had no idea where he was, nor did I have a way to ask anyone. But he did. My husband showed up and relayed what the surgeon had told us. We had three choices: surgery here with the resulting death from lack of post-operative care, second-rate Jerusalem hospital with who knows what outcome, or to try to get to the best surgeon in an Israeli hospital. It didn't take more than a couple of seconds to say we would do anything to get him into the best—if we could.

That started a whole cascade of impossibilities. The first would be getting in touch with the surgeon and getting the hospital to take our case. The next would be obtaining all the permissions needed by the ambulance, the driver, and the doctor. The final obstacle would be getting a newborn baby without documentation (no passport or I.D.) into one of the most secure places on earth—Israel.

The surgeon in Gaza phoned the surgeon in Israel. He understood our case and eased our way into the hospital. They would be expecting us if we could arrange everything else. My husband would spend the next four hours running around getting signatures, arranging for a driver, and getting a doctor who agreed to come with us. We did it. Ok, actually he did it. He was Superman. He had been able to move heaven and earth. In the meantime, I had gone home and packed a bag for both of us, grabbed our passports, and told my in-laws to 'watch' my three older children. I also grabbed what little cash we had on hand. It was a tearful goodbye, but I knew the children were in good hands and I needed to be with my baby.

Miraculously, and I don't use that term lightly, we were able to arrange for the Palestinian ambulance, a Palestinian driver, and a Palestinian doctor to accompany us. We had the necessary paperwork, but the doctor didn't look all that hopeful. We knew what was wrong, but if he started one of those coughing attacks, we weren't equipped to handle it. So, we needed to get there as soon as possible. Possible here was the keyword.

We drove with lights and sirens blaring. We made good time to Erez, the border between Gaza and Israel. We pulled in and had to have the entire ambulance gone over with a fine-tooth comb. I stayed with the baby and the doctor in the back while my husband and the driver got out and gave our papers to the checkpoint people. They knew we had a very sick baby, and would you believe, it took half an hour to scour our ambulance and check our papers. We were all set to leave when a soldier casually asked the driver for his I.D. card. The driver started to search his pockets and the ambulance, and then he got very anxious as he couldn't find it. He said he just had it as he had to turn it in when we arrived. He couldn't find it anywhere. He ran to the office, and they said they didn't have it. He searched everywhere. How does a card go missing when he had had it just moments ago? After about five minutes of searching, I was losing my patience. After ten minutes, I became hysterical.

I climbed out of the ambulance and started screaming and shouting. I caused so much noise, that a woman soldier finally confessed, "Oh, I have it here in my pants pocket." She had had it the whole time and didn't give it to us until I had gone postal! I would later hear shocking horror stories of the same abuse at Erez, and other checkpoints.

Thank God, we were back on the road again, only about an hour away. I wish. We had left the hospital around five o'clock in the afternoon. My son was exactly twenty-four hours old. By the time we left the checkpoint, it was closer to six o'clock. The significance of this is that we would run into 'rush-hour' traffic the closer we got to Tel Aviv. But even before that, we would face an unbelievable obstacle.

As I said earlier, we were traveling with lights and sirens. We were clearly a Palestinian ambulance trying to go as fast as possible. My husband was up front sitting next to the driver. We were slowing down. My husband explained that Israeli cars were pulling in front of us and deliberately slowing down and would you believe laughing while doing it? I wouldn't trust it either if I hadn't seen it with my own eyes. It wasn't one, but several cars did this. I also believe we had a guardian angel looking out for us because you won't accept as true what happened next.

An Israeli fire truck pulled out onto the freeway. Why is that such a miracle? Because the cars got out of his way. We pulled up behind the fire truck and even in rush-hour traffic, we made good time. In a host of miracles, this was just one. We followed it as far as we could, then took the turn off to Ramlah. Ramlah was about half an hour east of Tel Aviv.

When the ambulance pulled into the emergency department of Ashof Erofeh Hospital, I felt I could at least breathe a bit easier. I expected them to take my son directly to the NICU. That wasn't our first stop. The nurses indicated that we had to make a stop first. You will never believe where it was. We had to go to the cashier. I'm not kidding. We were directed to where it was and stood holding our dying son waiting to make payment arrangements. We had a little over two thousand dollars which we gave up directly. We also had a credit card which they insisted on taking an imprint of so that they could charge to it later. We gladly gave up everything we had, but please hurry.

When all the financial arrangements had been made, they finally took him into the NICU. We waited for what seemed forever (it was actually a couple of hours) before a nurse finally came out to talk to us. The nurse started with my pregnancy.

The first question was, "Were there any ultrasounds done?"

"Yes," I answered. Had there been any indication of any problems? Anything show up on the ultrasound? I answered no to all this line of questioning. If there had been any problems, we would have been much better prepared.

The question that finally made sense was, "Did you have too much amniotic fluid?" To which I, of course, answered yes. "Aha," said the nurse. At the time I had no idea what the 'aha' moment was but would learn all about 'hydrometriosis' (too much amniotic fluid) and why that was the clearest indicator that there was a problem. Remember what I said about the baby drinking the fluid in utero? They can't if the esophagus ends in a blind pouch—nowhere to go.

When they finally let us in to see our son, it was during the 'visiting' hour. I could hardly see the baby from all the tubes and wiring. We were with him only a short time when the surgeon showed up. All I could think of was, this is an Israeli, and my son is a Palestinian. I needed the surgeon to see my son as a person, so I said, "This is my son, Adam." The surgeon understood immediately what I was trying to say because he went on to explain that he was the one who had not only trained the surgeon in Gaza but had visited Shifa Hospital to do that training. He said that he wouldn't know exactly what was going on with our son until he got him open, but he was hopeful.

By the time we left the NICU, I had been up for thirty-six hours straight, scared to death, and had given birth. We were met by a Moroccan nurse who didn't speak any English, so she communicated with my husband in Arabic. She said, "You go home." I must have looked like death warmed over because she said again, "You go home." I had my husband tell her that first, we couldn't go home because that was Gaza, and it was too far away to start with. Second, we couldn't be sure to get back into Israel, and third, I wasn't leaving my baby. So, then she started to tell my husband that he should go home. But for the same reasons, he couldn't just go and come back. In point of fact, we were at least half an hour from any hotel accommodations, and we couldn't afford a taxi every time we wanted to come to the hospital. After about 10 minutes of trying to convince her, we weren't going anywhere, she went off to check.

Eventually, we were given a hospital room where I slept on a bed, and my husband slept in a chair. It was a private room, and had a bathroom and would you believe, a shower? We would be shuffled around the hospital, staying in a room for a few days at a time until they needed it for a patient. We needed five minutes to pack every time they moved us as we didn't have very much. It's amazing to me how little we actually needed.

After checking in the first night, we were actually allowed to visit Adam only twice a day for about half an hour at a time. The rest of the time was spent wandering around the hospital grounds, eating what food we could scrounge off the food carts left for families—both yogurt and cheese or meat-based sandwiches, but neither together as this was a highly kosher hospital. Meat and dairy actually require separate kitchens in a truly kosher house. We eventually found a small grocery store just down the road from the hospital within walking distance. At one point, we had to walk past a toy/gift shop to get to the grocery store, and I couldn't bear to look at the toys or newborn clothes as we didn't know for certain that Adam would make it. That had to be the hardest moment…when we just didn't know.

The first hurdle was the blood test for clotting factor. Adam didn't have any. If they tried to do any surgery, he had a very good chance of bleeding out on the table. So that was the first thing they had to fix. This took a couple of days, but in the meantime, he had developed full-blown pneumonia. The surgeon told us that it was most ideal to get these babies in the first twelve hours as this staves off the complications of pneumonia. We explained, of course, that we had no idea there was any problem, and that the x-ray tech had actually screwed up the first x-ray.

So now we had the clotting factor semi-fixed, at least they were hopeful he wouldn't bleed out. The pneumonia wouldn't be fixed until they could get the stomach detached from the lungs. This was the first surgery. It wasn't a long surgery, and he seemed to come through it well. It would be another five days before they would try the connection from the stomach to the esophagus.

Remember we were all alone, in a strange place where we were automatically known as strangers and by some as 'the enemy.' We were far from our children and from the rest of the family. It was a very lonely time. We had only each other to cling to.

I made one of the hardest phone calls of my life to my parents to let them know all about what we were going through. I reminded my mother about her telling me about the ambulance ride from Twin Falls to Salt Lake City, and about how I turned blue. I told her I didn't need to have seen it live to know the hell I had put her through. I thought it was a miracle I had a brother because I didn't know if I could have gone to have more after this. She reminded me how brave and strong I had been, and she had no doubt that my son would be just as strong.

In the middle of this chaos, we ran into an Israeli Arab family while we were waiting for the first surgery. Their son was having surgery to repair a cranial shunt for his hydrocephalus. The boy's shunt had become blocked, and if they didn't get it fixed right away, he could suffer brain damage. They were so welcoming and friendly to us when they found out we were from Gaza. They, of course, had never been to Gaza but had friends from there.

We were still worried about Adam but could only see him once in the morning and once in the afternoon, so we spent the rest of the day trying not to worry. That meant, of course, we did. They were most insistent that we come to lunch with them. Actually, we were quite tired of the hospital food, and there were no restaurants near the hospital, so taking a taxi was out of the question. We had no idea how long we would be here, and we had to conserve every penny.

Adam was recovering from the disconnection surgery. He had pneumonia and they didn't want to try to re-connect too early. That and they wanted to get his clotting factor up as well. It would be a few days, and he was getting better. So, we took a chance and went away from the hospital for a few hours. The nurses' station had our mobile number, and we wouldn't be far.

They were such a warm and welcoming family. They fed us a huge family dinner. They had invited the whole family over and we were the guests of honor. We ate too much, we laughed too much. We didn't have a seriously ill child for a little while. It was good. Over the years, I learned that we need to laugh and cry in the middle of great sadness. We would do that many times over the years when we lost a loved one. But thankfully, this wasn't one of those times when we lost a loved one, at least not yet.

They wanted us to sleep over, but we couldn't bear the thought of being away for that long. How could we ever forgive ourselves if we weren't there? We went back to the hospital. It almost felt like a prison. We couldn't leave, we couldn't enjoy ourselves, we couldn't even think about the future. How can you plan for your child's future when you don't even know if they will survive the next week? How can you buy baby clothes? A stroller? A car seat? We bought nothing. We were stuck. We couldn't even explore Tel Aviv or any other city. It was a very depressing time.

Finally, it was time to try the connection surgery. It is called an 'anastomosis.' literally, connecting two parts. The doctor wouldn't know anything until he had Adam cracked open. I remember watching all kinds of surgery on the T.V., but only almost passing out once. I watched them crack open a baby on its side. It looked so much like how my scar is, I almost passed out. All I could imagine was that they were doing this to Adam.

We waited in the surgical waiting room. It seemed like forever. The Arab man with the sick child came and waited with us for a little while. What can you say? What can you do? All I could think about was having dinner with my husband and his uncle and the uncle's wife. We were at a restaurant on the beach, and I was about seven months pregnant. I looked up at all the stars in the sky—not much light interference. I love the stars. My grandfather taught me some of the constellations. He knew them all and at one time he even had a telescope and would go out into the desert to watch the stars. I know you'll think me crazy, but I distinctly heard a voice say, "It's going to be alright." I don't claim it to be a dead relative or even God, but someone spoke to me, and I knew it was about my baby. I clung to that hope with all my strength. But then the surgeon came out of the doors.

His face was flat. No expression at all. I knew my son was dead. Oh God, he didn't make it. Then the surgeon opened his mouth. "It went just as expected, and the anastomosis was long enough. He's fine." What did he just say? The look on his face didn't match up with his words at all and I was still processing the face, not listening to the words. My son was fine? Is that what he had just said? Oh God, he was fine. Not out of danger but survived the surgery.

Remember that post-operative care was critical to survival as per the surgeon in Gaza? It would be here too, but they had a NICU and equipment and nurses. Actually, there were no complications, but he couldn't be released until he had been able to if not nurse, I was still trying, to at least suck a bottle.

If you've never nursed a baby, I can't describe the intimate feeling of giving everything a baby needs in a liquid form. They make blood, bones, muscle, neurons, and fingernails from this one substance, and I, as a mother, can produce it! The human body is quite miraculous, and its ability to recover and regenerate is beyond compare or comprehension.

It would be another 10 days before we would be able to actually go home, but it was the most bittersweet homecoming. You see, shortly after Adam was born, my mother-in-law's father passed away. He had asked about our son because we had named him Adam, and Adam was his younger brother's name, so he was very keen to know about him. It really was the circle of life in action.

You would think my story should end with this happy family reunion, then you would be so mistaken, my reader.

June 1996

We would need to take Adam back for a follow-up/check-up to see the doctor at the hospital. By now, Netanyahu had been elected and there was more trouble in Tel Aviv. I can't describe the humiliation the soldiers put critically ill people through as they tried to seek medical attention in Israel. We joined their company. Just imagine fully geared-up soldiers with an M-16 on their shoulder (not on safety) examining your medical papers just to see if you will be allowed to cross into their area and seek medical treatment. Oh, but these aren't just soldiers, they are fully qualified doctors! Yes, doctors with guns. I'd heard of doctors without borders, but never, doctors with guns! What, they shoot you then sew you back up?

They didn't want to let anyone in, but in the end, we all got through. Do you know how sick you have to be to be let in? Almost dying. Thank God, we weren't in that category, and actually, the doctor examining our paper had to call another doctor to make sure our need was 'real.' He'd never seen someone with Adam's problem, especially, not trying to cross the border. Remember what the Gaza surgeon had said? They die in Gaza.

We saw the doctor, and he said everything looked good. Adam was gaining weight, and I had to watch the gastrostomy tube he still had going into his stomach. They had to feed him from that until he recovered from the second surgery, but he was doing fine. Ok. I had to watch it. I was told to put a piece of tape across it, to keep the milk from coming back out, but otherwise, it was fine. It wasn't fine when during a routine bath, the plastic tube just fell out into the tub! I freaked out. I could see right into my son's stomach; I had a wet baby that was slipping and sliding all over. My daughter claims I was hysterical. Ok, maybe a bit. I got the baby out of the tub and dialed the doctor. He answered, thankfully. He said that that was actually a good thing. A good thing? It meant that my son was growing and had grown out of the G-tube. Just put a piece of tape over the gaping hole. A piece of tape? Are you kidding? What about closing it up? Surgery? Getting him back to see you? None of those were necessary.

Remember what I said about the body being a miraculous self-healing machine? Would you believe that the hole actually filled itself in? No need to do anything except cover it. Yes, my son would have a really ugly-looking scar, but I had lived with really ugly scars too. He would get over it! This is the one time my son actually differed from me. I never had a G-tube, so I think that's why I freaked out so badly. I had had no stories to warn me what to expect. No family reunions where they retold the story again and again.

Whew! Life is good. Actually, life felt pretty normal, but you know what they say about 'normal.' There is no such thing.

October 1996

At around six months old, you introduce solid food to a baby. It's the normal thing to do. They need the extra calories to grow. I started to feed Adam mushed-up peas, carrots, and rice the normal baby food items. Because by now it was headed to winter, avocados were in season and cheap. I mean really cheap. I started to feed Adam these nice green vegetables. This was long before it was thought to be a 'superfood.' He started to cough and choke. At one point, he was turning blue. Oh my God! Are you kidding? What the hell is wrong now? It had been too long and couldn't be a fistula like mine, could it? No. So what in the world was it?

First, we had to get the baby breathing. After he was rushed to the ER. They put him in the intensive care unit. I wasn't crazy. He was very bad and critical. They had no idea why. Nothing made sense. We were allowed to see him for a few minutes, and the look he gave his father—why did you allow them to do this to me? It melted our hearts when we had to leave him hooked up to so many machines; we couldn't see his tiny body. At least he wasn't intubated. The doctor really didn't want to do that if he didn't have to, and he said he'd wait 24 hours and see. You won't believe what happened in the next 24 hours. He was released from the ICU. Yes, you read right. He was released because he had improved so much. No one gets released from ICU, but he did, and more than once!

He would eat something, cough, choke, not breathe to the point that we even arranged for an oxygen tank in our house so I could get him breathing again. By about the fourth time, I was panicking. The doctors had no clue what was going on. Remember I said there wasn't even a CT machine in Gaza, let alone an MRI which is what he really needed!

He was dying—again! I called my parents desperate for help. I said I was coming home and if I had to declare bankruptcy, I would, just to get my son treated. My father actually pulled out the phone book (remember this is 1996—no cell phones or internet like now yet) and was thinking of calling pediatricians. My mother remembered a colleague of hers who had children treated at a children's hospital not too far away and told my father to hold off a bit. The colleague turned out to be a lifesaver—literally. I got a phone call and a fax from no less than the CEO of the children's hospital saying they would take Adam gratis if I could get him there. They couldn't provide transportation, but all other expenses would be free.

Great, now all I have to do is get me and my son out of Gaza, again! He at least had a passport so that was the easy part, right? Wrong. By now the situation in Israel had deteriorated to a bloody mess. Bombings and killings had closed the border. No way to even try and get to see the doctor. Hence the phone calls to my family. I had nowhere else to go, but home. And the only way home was to go to Tel Aviv Airport! Easy-peasy. Not!

At least this time it was only me and a sick baby, not an ambulance and driver plus a doctor. After four trips to the ICU and discharge from the same, we were desperate and scared. The doctors had no clue and I had only one hope to get out of there and go home.

I had the paper saying Adam had been accepted as a patient in the hospital in Utah; getting out of the Gaza Strip in 1996 was another matter. It actually took me calling the American Embassy and threatening to tell the entire world how they let an American citizen die and didn't lift a finger to get me out. I can be forceful when needed (remember the border trying to get him to the first surgery?) and this was needed. Great, we can get out. We were booked on a KLM flight and Adam had a cannula (a needle left in his hand so I could administer a drug [God only knows what the drug was, I believe it must have been adrenaline, but to this day I have no idea] in a syringe) in case he stopped breathing. Right, I can do this.

We got all the way to the airport, and the ticket counter took one look at Adam and the cannula and freaked out. Where were my medical authorization letters? What letters? It turns out that if someone is flying with a medical condition, the airline needed to know that in advance, and not just that, they wanted to have oxygen available just in case as well as the proper filled-out forms. Well, none of that was going to happen in the next hour, I can tell you. So, I ended up having to spend the night in an airport hotel room. At least it wasn't the lawn in front of the airport sign! Been there done that one!

But I couldn't sleep knowing that Adam could stop breathing at any time. How could I sleep? So, I stayed up all night drifting in and out of sleep. Got up and went to catch our 24-hour flight home. I don't remember much about that flight which means it was very uneventful. I did however get comfort from knowing I had a syringe and tank full of oxygen if I needed them. Thankfully, I didn't need either one!

It has become the story of legend how I pushed Adam toward my mother in a stroller and I ran into my father's arms and cried like a baby. I was home and I would be taken care of. But first, we had to take Adam to the hospital. We arrived and they had been waiting for us. They checked him in and whisked him into the pediatric ICU. His symptoms were troubling, and they didn't have any more of a clue than we'd had in Gaza. The nurse turned to me and said, "You go home." Deja vu all over again! But this time I took her advice and went home to sleep. I must have looked like death warmed over—again!

The next day, he was scheduled for an MRI, but they were very concerned as to get a good picture you need the patient to lie flat for almost half an hour. Good luck getting a six-month-old baby to do that! They were also worried that anesthesia would trigger a non-breathing attack, so we were stuck. What to do? They had faced this same situation many times and suggested giving only a partial dose of anesthesia, as opposed to a full dose. Just enough to calm him down and hold still while they took pictures.

I had only heard about MRI and never really understood what it did until I was called into the imaging room by the x-ray technician. She was very patient and explained how it was aligning the cells and then the computer rearranged the pictures it took so we could see them. It was amazing. She had a scroll mouse, and it was showing slices of the interior of my son. She rolled it up and down showing me his trachea. One minute, it was a round circle and then the next as she rolled down, it kept getting smaller and smaller till it was almost shut! What? How can he breathe if it goes down to nothing?

Ok, so now we knew what was wrong, what were we going to do to fix this? I would meet with two surgeons; one who wanted to do open heart surgery (basically exploratory) and the other who suggested a more conservative approach by doing what's called an aortopexy. Basically, it involves attaching the trachea to the breastbone to keep it open. It isn't a complicated surgery and if it worked, we would know right away. No more choking spells.

And because this was a children's hospital connected to a university teaching hospital, could they videotape the procedure as it wasn't that common?

I agreed to both, the aortopexy and the taping. The video wasn't very long, a couple of minutes at most. It shows Adam's trachea from the inside. One minute it's flat, and the next it's wide open. Flat then open, flat then open. The surgeon explained that every time he pulled up on the trachea to attach it is when he was open and when he would let go, it flopped down like a soft piece of bologna.

What I found most interesting about the whole procedure was when the U.S. surgeon asked who had done the anastomosis. He commented that it was very skillful and quite efficient. I told him about the surgeon in Israel and he said that not only was he the greatest in the Middle East, but in all of Europe. After I got back to Gaza, I called this great surgeon and told him what we had done in Utah, and he said that the U.S. surgeon was the best in the entire United States.

My son had had the two best surgeons in the entire world work on him. Now if that isn't a miracle, I don't know what is. He went back to the United States at four years old for a check-up with the doctor just to make sure he was growing fine, etc. They found a blip on his EKG. But it turned out to be a round heart, not shaped like a normal one, so he'll always have that blip. But otherwise, he's a healthy, happy man; married with children now. Talk about a happy ending.

Present Day

I want to add an addendum to my story. I hadn't planned on writing about it now, but I feel it necessary.

I have visited many times since and would love to write about those but feel it wouldn't serve the greater purpose. We arrived in several non-conventional ways. But I would like to write about spending most of 2020 in Gaza.

We went for an engagement party and stayed for a pandemic. Remember the brother-in-law who was blown up by the Israelis? It was his oldest son, and my husband and his brothers who were abroad, thought it was a good idea to be present for his engagement.

I was out of yet another job, and my husband didn't have any pressing engagements either. We figured we could visit for roughly a month, and then come home and figure out what to do with our lives.

December 2020

It took over two days to get to a place that is about four hours by car with no stops. In the process, we lost a couple of items that were confiscated as being 'contraband' by the Egyptian army. But made our way to wait at the border to be the last ones processed. Remember, my husband doesn't have a residency card, but this was one of the few times when a first-degree relative could get you in. We were with not one, but two of his brothers. I had been warned about this procedure, and even brought our marriage license just for this occasion. Not the worst time ever, but not the easiest either.

Gaza—Again

I hugged everyone. They were all waiting patiently on the Palestinian side. I even hugged a reluctant teenage nephew. He was quite shocked to get a hug from a woman he didn't even know. But I didn't care. I hugged his father, and that went a long way in easing his hesitancy. I couldn't believe we were actually back where it all started so many years ago.

The drive home was a blur, but we met so many people at the border and even more waiting at the building. I was home. We were home. We had a home to come to. Others aren't that lucky. During the various wars—that doesn't even make sense. Wars are fought by semi-equal parties. This is an industrial war machine against rock-throwing juveniles or homemade rockets at best. No guidance systems, no early warning detection, just your home blown to bits and everyone in it, and possibly the neighbors as well. So many men, women, and children blown to bits—for what? Land that doesn't even belong to them?

We were home, and home for a very good reason. To celebrate the engagement of the oldest son of the martyred brother. My husband would stand in the place of the brother. Only one problem, I didn't know there was going to be a huge party in two days. Remember how these parties were not just for the participants but for the entire city?

I needed a party dress and fast. Yes, we had a house full of furniture, and appliances, including a working stove and fridge, and even a bed, but a befitting party dress? No. So, when in Rome, go shopping!

We went to one of the most exclusive and expensive shops in the city. We walked in and just so happened that the mother of the groom (my sister-in-law, the widow) needed to pick up the dress that had been tailored for her from this store. I was waiting for her to retrieve her dress when out of nowhere this man asked, "How are you, Mrs. Adria?" Say what? The only people to ever call me that were students. He continued, "You don't remember me, do you?" To be honest I had no clue who this 40-year-old man was. And do use my first name was rather cheeky if you ask me. He said, "I was in your seventh-grade class at the private school." I don't do math very well, but that was over 27 years ago! OMG. I really had no clue who he was, but he had remembered me fondly. Needless to say, I bought a very nice dress and negotiated a very good discount based on my very old reputation and memory.

March 2020

Can you say coronavirus?

The engagement party was so much fun, we decided to stay for the wedding. It would be 7 March and we had permission to leave on 15 March. We had been following the news, but not too closely. Weddings were still taking place; borders were still open, although they were now checking people coming in for something called COVID-19 whatever that was.

The wedding was a huge success, and we had such a good time. Within a week, everything would be shut down. No gatherings, no parties, no leaving. What do you mean by no leaving? The border closed on 13 March. You can't make that up. We missed it by two days.

We didn't panic. I wasn't losing my job, we had a house, a bed, and more, we had family. We had arranged for a professional archaeologist to take us on a tour of Gaza City. She would go on to become a very special friend. We rented a bus and took the entire family out for the day. It will always be a special memory for all of us. She showed us places that most of the family didn't even know about—they passed by every day but didn't even think to inquire about.

April 2020

We would spend Ramadan with the family and all the special memories that conjured up from the years we'd lived there and done that.

By now, I was getting a bit panicked. They said the border would open after Ramadan. It didn't. A niece and her husband had spent a month in quarantine trying to get back in after visiting Cairo for three days seeking a Canadian visa.

But we had no 'Rona.' None. There were no wedding parties allowed, but life continued on as normal or as near normal as possible.

We went to the beach during the day to swim, or just listen to the waves. We went to the beach at night to watch the stars. We went to the grocery store, restaurants, and ice cream shop. I would teach the entire building how to crochet and even some friends. I would spend my time teaching ESL at the local orphanage to staff and teachers by volunteering my time. Life was pretty normal. I am sure there wasn't even one case of COVID-19 in the whole of the Gaza Strip. How do I know? Because it would devastate this closed area with no access to good vaccines only one week after we eventually got out.

August 2020

I had accepted a position, literally sight unseen, to be a principal in Florida. I'd only been to Florida once, and it was very nice. Would I like to move there and work? Why not? It has a beach, and good weather, except for the occasional hurricane. I had been working remotely for almost two months trying to set up schedules, hire teachers, and get the school ship shape—all from my computer in Gaza. Not a mean feat, let me tell you. I showed up literally the day before school started and was able to greet my teachers and students on the first day of the school year!

Writing

I am not sure exactly how to tell you this, dear reader, but every word of the above is true. I have lived every moment and detail you've read. It has taken me over four years to write this because I've had to relive each and every moment. Some are such joy, and some are so much sorrow that I've taken breaks for months at a time because I relived the trauma. But in the end, I'm very glad to share, if you can believe it, just a bit of my story.

There are other pieces I can't talk about now. Adventures that would make your hair stand on end because they are so fantastic. Let's just say, over and under and leave it at that. I may write about them someday and they are the stuff of family lore. But above all else, I have come to love my family and the people of Gaza. I can only hope that they embrace me as much as I have them.